"I have found this book extremely helpful, especially in understanding my own reactions to Marginal Catholics and being able to critique those reactions. I have insisted that all members of our pastoral staff read it. It has also been a great help to tuning in to the 'teachable' moments of our evangelization."

— *Fr. Dan Danielson*, Pastor,
St. Augustine Parish, Pleasanton, California

"*The Marginal Catholic* is an excellent book because it deals with what's happening today in the lives of our people. It deals with reality... since there are an estimated 15 million alienated, unchurched, marginal Catholics, it is a blessing to have this book to help handle the situations that will surely arise in pastoral ministry today." — *The Cord*

"Any minister remotely connected to sacramental preparation should in conscience make time to read this landmark book. *The Marginal Catholic* is characterized by sensitivity and realness and based on the fruit of a lifetime of pastoral work and research."

— *National Catholic Reporter*

THE MARGINAL CATHOLIC

For Henry

with warm memories
and prayerful best
wishes for your
work at the
Cathedral

Joe Chang
1/6/02.

The Marginal Catholic
Challenge, Don't Crush

JOSEPH M. CHAMPLIN

REVISED AND UPDATED EDITION
with references to the *Catechism of the Catholic Church*

ALBA·HOUSE   NEW·YORK

SOCIETY OF ST. PAUL, 2187 VICTORY BLVD., STATEN ISLAND, NEW YORK 10314

ST PAULS

Library of Congress Cataloging-in-Publication Data

Champlin, Joseph M.
  The marginal Catholic : challenge, don't crush / Joseph M. Champlin. — Rev. and
updated ed.
    p. cm.
  Includes bibliographical references and index.
  ISBN 0-8189-0882-3 (alk. paper)
    1. Church work with ex-church members — Catholic Church. 2 Catholic
Church — Membership. 3. Catholic converts. I. Title.

  BX2347.8.E82 C43 2000
  282—dc21

                                                                    00-033153

Nihil Obstat:
✠ Most Rev.Thomas J. Costello, DD
Censor Deputatus

Imprimatur:
✠ Most Rev. James M. Moynihan, DD
Bishop of Syracuse

The Nihil Obstat and Imprimatur are official declarations that a book or
pamphlet is free of doctrinal error. No implication is contained therein
that those who have granted the Nihil Obstat and Imprimatur agree with
the contents, opinions or statements expressed.

Produced and designed in the United States of America by the
Fathers and Brothers of the Society of St. Paul,
2187 Victory Boulevard, Staten Island, New York 10314-6603,
as part of their communications apostolate.

ISBN: 0-8189-0882-3

Printing Information:

Current Printing - first digit   1   2   3   4   5   6   7   8   9   10

Year of Current Printing - first year shown

2001   2002   2003   2004   2005   2006   2007   2008   2009   2010

Table of Contents

Foreword
to the Revised Edition

$\mathcal{A}$ decade has passed since the initial version of this book appeared on the scene. During those ten years, I conducted about 50 workshops for clergy and pastoral ministers in the United States and Canada on the theme and content of this volume.

At some point in each conference the assembled people divided into groups of three or four and pondered these questions:

* Have you ever experienced a situation in which persons considered to be marginal Catholics sought baptism or marriage?

* How did you feel at that time about this challenging encounter?

* What was your pastoral response?

This process always generated energetic discussions and active participation by every individual present.

These issues were very real then and continue to trouble parish leaders today, although perhaps to a slightly less degree. Do I or don't I baptize? Should I agree to the wedding of this problematic couple or send them away? Do the parents have faith and will the child be raised as a Catholic? Are the engaged couple believers and will their marriage last?

Several historical, pastoral and theological principles emanating from the Second Vatican Council in the 1960's led the clergy first and, after, pastoral ministers as well, to those sometimes anxious self-questionings. We could summarize them in this way:

* The sacraments are acts of faith; they presuppose and require faith.

* Active, conscious and informed participation is necessary for the sacramental rites to have their full or maximum effect.

* The Eucharist has become more and more central to Catholic worship and life.

* All the sacraments possess a communal, an ecclesial and a wider Church dimension.

* The sacramental celebration should work or have a successful outcome: for example, the infant is educated and formed in the Catholic tradition or, another illustration, the marriage lasts.

Marginal, fringe or inactive Catholics who are the main subjects of this book usually fall short in all or most of these categories.

Their faith (perhaps, better, the manifestation of it) is weak or practically non-existent; their understanding of and participation in the liturgy is minimal; their attendance at Sunday Mass is rare; their connection with the parish is very tenuous at best; the prospects of the parents raising the children as Catholics and the couple living a life-long Christian marriage are in the mind of the clergy or pastoral minister, dim at best.

The Marginal Catholic: Challenge, Don't Crush was written to provide supportive principles and practical suggestions for those in the parish who often face these troublesome situations. This current updated and slightly revised edition includes all the information in the first volume and also contains at the end of each chapter some pertinent paragraphs from the *Catechism of the Catholic Church*.

Those fifty conferences also surfaced new insights and other issues.

One participant, for example, suggested additional questions for the warm welcome and cordial introductory element of the first interview with couples described in my book. I had suggested as icebreakers: Where do you work? How did you meet? What were your first impressions? When did you become engaged?

The added inquiries are: How did he propose? You have decided to marry: Why him? Why her? What made you choose to be married in the Catholic Church? Why this particular church?

The additional questions reveal much about the couple. Moreover, they often trigger tender responses as the engaged pair mutually articulate the lovable qualities which they see in each other.

In most of the conferences, participants likewise raised the increasingly frequent issue of couples living together before marriage. How, they asked, do we best respond pastorally to that situation?

Neither the first nor this revised edition of *The Marginal Catholic* deals specifically with that challenge. However, there are several contemporary resources which do and should be most helpful to pastoral ministers.

Faithful To Each Other Forever: A Catholic Handbook of Pastoral Help for Marriage Preparation issued by the U.S. Bishops Committee for Pastoral Research and Practices (United States Catholic Conference Publishing Services, Washington, DC, 1988). A six-page section on "The Question of Cohabitation" provides empirical data, theological insights and pastoral suggestions.

"Marriage Preparation and Cohabitating Couples: Information Report" issued in August, 1999 by the National Conference of Catholic Bishops' Committee on Marriage and Family (*Origins*, CNS Documentary Service, Catholic News Service, Washington, DC, September 16, 1999, Volume 29: No. 14). This offers a thorough update of *Faithful To Each Other Forever* with massive statistical information and many pastoral recommendations.

Living Together: Questions and Answers Regarding Cohabitation and the Church's Moral Teaching. This small, colorful booklet issued by the Bishops of Pennsylvania in September, 1999 has been designed for distribution to the couples themselves (Pennsylvania Catholic Conference, Harrisburg, PA, 1999).

Together for Life (Ave Maria Press, Notre Dame, Indiana, Sixth Revised Edition, 1997). A commentary on "Living Together" repeats in summary and succinct form current statistics, reasons why cohabitation may not be the best way to prepare for marriage, and repeats questions from *Faithful To Each Other Forever* for the couples to ponder about their living together.

The rector of a mid-western Cathedral suggests to cohabitating couples that, if in their judgment they cannot stop living together, they nevertheless plan to remain sexually inactive for a time span before the marriage. In that way, he observes, the night of the wedding will not be the same as the night before the wedding. This priest draws a parallel between his recommendation and the Lenten practice of self-sacrifice, in which we give up something for a short period of time in order to gain a higher goal.

Father Andrew Greeley, well known author and sociologist, writing in *America*, (November 20, 1999), urges parish leaders to "invite, charm and enchant the laity as they approach the sacraments instead of imposing rules and regulations, creating obstacles and demanding compliance."

In many ways, his remarks capture the tone and theme of *The Marginal Catholic*. The initial edition helped many parish clergy and pastoral leaders over the past decade respond in such a consistent, but compassionate fashion to "marginal" Catholics seeking the sacraments. I am grateful to Father Edmund C. Lane, S.S.P., of Alba House for his willingness to publish this revised and updated version. I pray that it will continue in the years ahead to assist others with an often demanding and perplexing challenge.

Introduction

*I*n Oklahoma, a woman called upon the parish priest and asked him to baptize her grandchild, the infant of Catholics who were not actively practicing their faith. He responded, "When the parents start going to Mass on Sundays, then we will talk about the baptism."

In Florida, another non-practicing Catholic couple contacted the local pastor to arrange for their child's baptism. He worked out a time to meet with them in their own home, spoke to them about the meaning and obligations of baptism, then posed this question: "During the ceremony I will ask you in front of a large group of people, 'Are you willing to accept the responsibility of training this child in the practice of the faith?' Would you answer 'yes' to that inquiry?" They nodded affirmatively and agreed to attend the parish baptismal class.

Those examples represent two current approaches of parish priests and pastoral leaders when so-called marginal Catholics seek the sacrament of baptism.

In the first procedure, the clergy insist upon regular attendance at Mass, strong commitment to the Church and even registered membership in the parish as prerequisites. In the second, the parish priest or pastoral leaders discuss with the petitioner the Church's understanding of the sacrament, note the responsibilities which flow from that concept and urge fidelity to the ideal. But they do not demand prior church attendance as an essential condition.

In many conferences with the clergy throughout this country

and Canada over the past decade, I have found the issue of responding to marginal Catholics, especially those who request the sacrament of baptism and matrimony, to be a source of great concern
for persons in pastoral ministry.

On the other hand, parish leaders wish to follow the thrust
of the Second Vatican Council which teaches that the sacraments
are acts of faith that require and presuppose faith. Simply to pour
baptismal water or witness nuptial vows when the parents or couple
seem to possess little or no faith almost makes those actions magical rites, contrary to the entire spirit of the renewed liturgy.

On the other hand, the same leaders know that the Council
documents also teach that the sacraments nourish and deepen faith.
Their practical experience with people over the years has made them
realize that persons who have grown careless about their religion
often will discover those sacramental occasions to be moments of
grace which bring them back or closer to God.

The goal or ideal here is to challenge peripheral Catholics who
seek a baptism or marriage in the Church, but not to crush them.
Pastoral leaders wish to communicate with forceful, persuasive clarity what the Church expects of its members, yet they do not want
thereby to snuff out what may be but a weak flickering flame of
faith.

This book has been written primarily for those who wrestle
with these delicate and complex issues on a regular basis in parish
life. That includes priests and deacons, together with the many religious and lay persons involved in pastoral ministry today. However, I hope it also will prove of interest and value to parents,
couples, families and individuals whose lives have or will be touched
by these different approaches to the Church's sacraments.

In the past some people or their loved ones were creatively
challenged by a constructive and wise pastoral approach; others were
crushed by a well meaning, but too severe manner of ministering
sacramental rites. Perhaps that experience of being challenged or
crushed is happening to others at this very moment. Undoubtedly
it will happen to still others in the days ahead.

The first chapters of this volume discuss the approach of reaching out to marginal Catholics from biblical, legal, liturgical, psychological and theological points of view. The general principles discussed apply to all sacramental situations, not only to baptism and matrimony. As pastoral leaders understand so well, perplexing decisions about inactive Catholics likewise occur frequently in connection with first penance, first Eucharist, confirmation, anointing of the sick and Christian burial.

The last chapters consider specifically baptism and marriage. Readers with limited time available may feel impelled to rush ahead and pick those practical fruits of my reflection. I would simply caution that these particular applications, a few of which run contrary to current procedures in some Catholic parishes, flow naturally and logically from the more generic, theoretical discussions which precede them.

In the Concluding Summary we have drawn out the main points of every chapter in the book for readers who desire a general overview of its contents or seek to review rather swiftly the essential message of each section, particularly Chapters 1-6.

Each chapter begins with an actual human experience of being challenged or crushed by Church personnel during some encounter which involved the sacraments. All but two of them are excerpts from personal letters received in response to an appeal I made in an article about marginal Catholics, in *Our Sunday Visitor* (cf. Jan. 31, 1988 issue). Names have been omitted, but the letters' states of origin are indicated. Sources of the other two experiences are given in the footnotes.

This project and the publication resulting from it were made possible through the sabbatical policy for priests of my own Syracuse diocese and a generous grant from Our Sunday Visitor Institute. I am very grateful for both, and to the many who offered me assistance along the way. Details of my journey and the names of those diverse contributors can be found in the end section, Process and Acknowledgments.

Biblical Abbreviations

OLD TESTAMENT

Genesis	Gn	Nehemiah	Ne	Baruch	Ba
Exodus	Ex	Tobit	Tb	Ezekiel	Ezk
Leviticus	Lv	Judith	Jdt	Daniel	Dn
Numbers	Nb	Esther	Est	Hosea	Ho
Deuteronomy	Dt	1 Maccabees	1 M	Joel	Jl
Joshua	Jos	2 Maccabees	2 M	Amos	Am
Judges	Jg	Job	Jb	Obadiah	Ob
Ruth	Rt	Psalms	Ps	Jonah	Jon
1 Samuel	1 S	Proverbs	Pr	Micah	Mi
2 Samuel	2 S	Ecclesiastes	Ec	Nahum	Na
1 Kings	1 K	Song of Songs	Sg	Habakkuk	Hab
2 Kings	2 K	Wisdom	Ws	Zephaniah	Zp
1 Chronicles	1 Ch	Sirach	Si	Haggai	Hg
2 Chronicles	2 Ch	Isaiah	Is	Malachi	Ml
Ezra	Ezr	Jeremiah	Jr	Zechariah	Zc
		Lamentations	Lm		

NEW TESTAMENT

Matthew	Mt	Ephesians	Eph	Hebrews	Heb
Mark	Mk	Philippians	Ph	James	Jm
Luke	Lk	Colossians	Col	1 Peter	1 P
John	Jn	1 Thessalonians	1 Th	2 Peter	2 P
Acts	Ac	2 Thessalonians	2 Th	1 John	1 Jn
Romans	Rm	1 Timothy	1 Tm	2 John	2 Jn
1 Corinthians	1 Cor	2 Timothy	2 Tm	3 John	3 Jn
2 Corinthians	2 Cor	Titus	Tt	Jude	Jude
Galatians	Gal	Philemon	Phm	Revelation	Rv

THE MARGINAL CATHOLIC

1   Once a Catholic

*I*n the end, the good aspects of going to Catholic school outweighed the negative for me, and for several reasons. For one thing, I got a knowledge of English grammar out of it; for another thing, it gave me something to talk about — people love to hear those stories; third, it gave me something to believe in, in terms of the religious training. Nobody has anything to believe in anymore. I go to church every Sunday. I don't see how you can't believe in it. One day, I was having a cup of coffee in the Harvard Medical School cafeteria in Peter Ben Brigham (now Brigham and Women's) Hospital, and I was listening to four medical students talking. They were saying that the body was so complicated that it could not have just occurred by itself, that it had to come from a higher source. They all agreed on that. I just started laughing because, I mean, they should've just gone to grammar school with me and they would've known as much. I could've told them that.

The religious training that the nuns put into you in grammar school comes back in one instant to everyone who ever had it — no matter how far they get from the Church or how much they laugh about it with their friends. Let a guy have one chest pain, one twinge in the chest, and he goes flying back to the things that he was taught in third or fourth grade. Nobody leaves the Catholic

Church. Pete Hamill has fallen away — but he'll get a chest
pain, he'll be back, don't worry. People like him procras-
tinate with the religion, they walk away from it. They just
don't want to spend the time going to church.

—Jimmy Breslin[1]

Robert J. Fitzgerald spent his working years in the educational field,
serving, among other places, as principal of elementary schools on
Long Island and headmaster of a secondary school for the Near East
American Community in Beirut. Retired and burdened with slightly
impaired hearing, "Professor Fitz" came with clock-like regularity
to the 12:30 p.m. Sunday Mass at St. Joseph's Church in Camillus,
New York. With equal predictability this distinguished man claimed
a seat in the front row, south side, near the pulpit where he tried to
catch as much of the homily as possible.

Having read a description of my project concerning baptism
and matrimony, he asked one day after the liturgy, "What do you
mean by the term 'marginal Catholic'?"

It was a very perceptive inquiry and one that raises a host of
other questions which we will examine in the next few pages. At the
conclusion of the present chapter, I will give a precise definition of
"marginal Catholic" for the purpose of this book. But for the moment, let us explore Mr. Fitzgerald's questions with its multiple
ramifications.

By adding an adjective like "marginal" to the word Catholic,
we immediately enter into a world of comparisons. Thus, a marginal Catholic stands in contrast to what we might term a "mainstream" Catholic, an inactive Catholic to an active one, a non-practicing Catholic to a practicing one, and a bad or poor Catholic to a
good one. If we wish to use the expression with which Jimmy Breslin
labels his columnist colleague, Pete Hamill, we would in addition
compare a fallen-away Catholic to a faithful one.

Drawing such comparisons by categorizing people is, however,
a process at once risky and questionable, elusive and complex.

Making Judgments

It is risky and questionable because to affix adjectives describing a person's Catholicism means making judgments about an individual's inner life. Only God can and may do that. "Stop judging, that you may not be judged" (Mt 7:1). "Therefore, you are without excuse, every one of you who passes judgment" (Rm 2:1). "The one who judges me is the Lord. Therefore, do not make judgment before the appointed time, until the Lord comes, for he will bring to light what is hidden in darkness and will manifest the motives of our hearts, and then everyone will receive praise from God" (1 Cor 4:4-5).

We believe the Church possesses a divine element because it not only enjoys Christ's presence and protection, but also deals with our relationship with God, with the spiritual or interior lives of human beings. Nevertheless, the Creator alone can penetrate the depths of every person.

> O Lord, you have probed me and you know me;
> you know when I sit and when I stand;
> you understand my thoughts from afar...
> Such knowledge is too wonderful for me;
>   too lofty for me to attain (Ps 139:1-2,6).

Consequently, we should not, indeed cannot, judge or categorize the inner religious state of another individual.

Catholic Codes of Conduct

But the Church as established by Christ also possesses a human element because it is made up of flesh and blood, spirit and body members. They form a visible society or community with unique requirements for those who wish to enter, and specially given codes of conduct for those who belong.

Labeling Catholics as mainstream or marginal refers, therefore, merely to the observance or non-observance of those codes of conduct. Rules, even though governing religious or spiritual activities, pertain essentially to a person's exterior life. While their observance ought to and normally does flow out of and reflect an individual's inner state, that connection is not automatic. It is a barometer of one's interior condition, but not necessarily an accurate and precise measure of the existence or degree of a person's faith.

Thus, we acknowledge the biblical injunction against judging and recognize our inability as human beings to evaluate the inner life of another person. Moreover, while understanding the need for certain regulations of behavior within the Church as indispensable for a visible society, we at the same time grasp the imperfect connection between those external actions and an individual's interior life.

If those factors alone were not sufficient to make this judgment-making risky and questionable, there are more.

Pre-Vatican II Criteria of Catholicism

Prior to the Second Vatican Council, there were several commonly accepted norms used to distinguish good from bad or practicing from non-practicing Catholics: Sunday and holy day Mass, Easter duty confession and communion, Friday abstinence, Lenten fast, marriage in the Church and registration in the parish. Those who observed all these precepts were "good" and "practicing" Catholics; those who failed to observe them were "bad" and "non-practicing." The degree of badness and non-practice was measured by how many of the rules has been violated and for how long.

Sponsors for baptism or confirmation often were expected to obtain a certificate from their parish stating that they were "good, practicing Catholics." The definition of, or requirements for, such a Catholic varied from church to church and from priest to priest. Nevertheless, a set of questions about attending Sunday Mass and making one's Easter duty was the usual test to be passed, if the petitioner was to secure the signed form.

Post-Vatican II Decline in Criteria

During the decades since the Council, however, those rather easily recognizable norms significantly diminished or disappeared. Catholics now eat meat on Friday like everyone else except during Lent. Only Ash Wednesday and Good Friday are strict fast days. Almost all receive communion at Mass regardless of what they have done or not done. Many postpone confession for one, two, several or many years and still approach the altar for the Eucharist. Divorced and remarried couples in great numbers, with and without Church approbation, consider themselves good Catholics and do not hesitate to come forward for communion. In a mobile culture which also hinders long-term commitments, many persons go to Mass at places of choice rather than affiliate with the neighborhood church.

To get back to our original question, then, the external criteria for a mainstream as opposed to a marginal Catholic are less defined, reduced in practice to Mass attendance, frequent communion and registration in the parish. But even those lack the precision of yesteryear. The obligation of Mass every Sunday is questioned by some; many, as noted, receive communion regardless of previous omissions or commissions; and a certain percentage of Catholics prefers not to enroll in any parish.

All of these norms, regulations or standards for estimating a person's Catholicism deal with external practices. If they are, today, elusive and complex, how much more so are the determinants of an individual's faith, its very existence, and its degree.

Existence and Levels of Faith: Elusive Questions

What level of faith is needed for membership in the Church, for reception of a sacrament, for everlasting salvation? What type of acceptance of the Church's teachings is required to become a Catholic, to remain a Catholic, to be a faithful, good Catholic?

A few illustrations may emphasize the complexity and elusiveness of determining a person's faith and belief in the Church's teachings, as well as evaluating that individual's observance of its regulations.

Faith of Former Catholics

The introductory comments by Jimmy Breslin came from a book *Once a Catholic* which carries this descriptive subtitle: "Prominent Catholics and Ex-Catholics Discuss the Influence of the Church on Their Lives and Work." The author interviewed 26 relatively well-known people ranging from actor George Carlin to novelist Mary Gordon, from politician Eugene McCarthy to film maker Martin Scorsese. He then edited their remarks and added his observations. Some, like Breslin, are regular church-going Catholics. Others would echo Carlin's words, "I've been gone a long time now." However, few if any of those who say they have "fallen-away" or have "faded out from the whole thing" have become active, committed members of another religion or another religious tradition.[2]

It is interesting to speculate what Church affiliation those self-named ex-Catholics would give for themselves should they enter a hospital for major surgery or during serious illness. In my four decades of pastoral experience, I have found that persons who have not been active Catholics, even for many years, or who disagree with certain teachings of the Church, will still mark "Catholic" on the religious identification section of a health care admission form.

Too Far, Too Fast or Not Far or Fast Enough

This struggle over faith in the Church's teachings and adherence to its rules extends to groups on opposite ends of the Catholic ideological spectrum. Among both those who judge that the Church after the Second Vatican Council has moved too far, too fast, and those who judge it has progressed neither far, nor fast enough, are some who object to what the Church today tells us we must believe and do.

　* Archbishop Marcel Lefebvre has, for many years, personified the status of persons who reject the reforms and renewal of the Second Vatican Council. His opposition climaxed on June 30, 1988, when in direct, explicit defiance of Pope John Paul II, he ordained four men as bishops to carry on his Society of St. Pius X.

　In an exchange of letters between the Vatican and the archbishop prior to this precipitous act, Lefebvre explained his position to Pope John Paul II:

> It is in order to keep intact the faith in which we were baptized that we felt obligated to oppose the spirit of Vatican II and the reforms inspired by it.
>
> 　That false ecumenism which is the origin of all the innovations of the council — in the liturgy, in the new relations between the Church and the world, in the concept of the Church itself — is leading the Church to ruin and Catholics to apostasy.
>
> 　Radically opposed to this destruction of our faith and resolved to stay within the traditional doctrine and discipline of the Church, especially in that which concerns the training of priests and religious life, we feel the absolute need to have Church authorities who take up our concerns and help us to guard against the spirit of Vatican II and the spirit of Assisi.
>
> 　We shall continue to pray that modern Rome, infested by modernism, will once again become Catholic Rome and will once again find its 2,000-year-old tradition. Then the problem of reconciliation will no longer have a reason to exist, and the Church will find a new youth.[3]

What about the significant number of his followers around the world, who in disobedience to the pope and local bishops, each week participate in pre-Vatican II Tridentine Masses celebrated by

Lefebvre's priests or clergy in sympathy with him? What is the condition of their faith and their status in the Church?

    * If Archbishop Lefebvre judges that the Church in recent years has moved too far, too fast, "thirteen valiant women challenging the Church" think with equally strong convictions that it has not progressed far or fast enough. This quotation is actually the subtitle of a book, *The Inside Stories*, edited by Annie Lally Milhaven. It consists of interviews with critical Catholic feminists — five nuns and eight laywomen — some of whom are married, while others are single or divorced. Their objections to the Church are quite consistent, all of them seeing a patriarchal, hierarchical, institutional functioning within the Christian Church, which for them is ethically and theologically illegitimate, personally oppressive and sinfully violent.[4] They do recognize positive changes in the Catholic Church since Vatican II, but fear now a retreat from those forward steps. Moreover, these women argue that many enormous steps still need to be taken if true liberation is to occur.

    A few quotes from exchanges in the book will exemplify the unhappiness of some of these women with certain official Catholic teachings and practices, as well as their tenuous connections with the Church.

    "The institutional Church is not at the center of my life. I come in and go out of the institutional Church as I have more or less patience for it."

    "She spends no time or energy on what she visualizes as a currently perverted Church which has lost its sense of justice and love. Rather her creativity and lucidity is focused on constructing a theology for the future, a new church, women-church."

    "The person in charge of the liturgy or worship is the one in whose home we meet.... We call it a eucharist because that's what it is. It is eucharist, celebrated by the group gathered. We sometimes use the words of the institutional Church, sometimes not."

    "Church government is not divinely ordained, and I have no particular overriding respect for that government. It is not sacred and should not be treated as sacred."

"Be it the issues of abortion, ordination, birth control, homosexuality or any issue that is controversial at this time, I, as public witness, am not going to blindly and obediently be submissive to 'Church fathers' whose teachings are wrong and evil.... We clearly said to them we did not believe in the Roman Catholic position."

"I hope I'm at least among the people of God.... In terms of Church, whatever church means, I believe I am a person of faith."[5]

In parallel fashion to the case of Archbishop Lefebvre and his followers, but from diametrically opposed circumstances, we can raise a similar question: What about the faith and status in the Roman Catholic Church of these women and others who think or act like them?

Communal or Cafeteria Catholics

The phenomenon of "communal" or "cafeteria" Catholics has emerged quite strongly in the United States over the past couple of decades or so. There are people who pick and choose among major beliefs and practices of the Church and yet consider themselves "good" Catholics. They sense no obligations to accept Catholicism or the Catholic Church as a total indivisible package.

Such persons can find support from certain theologians like moralist Father Charles Curran who defends the thesis "that on some issues a loyal Catholic may disagree in theory and in practice with the Church's non-infallible teachings and still consider oneself a loyal and good Roman Catholic."[6]

Pope John Paul II disagrees. Speaking to the United States bishops in Los Angeles on September 16, 1987, he said,

> It is sometimes reported that a large number of Catholics today do not adhere to the teaching of the Church on a number of questions, notably sexual conjugal morality, divorce, and remarriage. Some are reported as not accepting the Church's clear position on abortion. It has also

been noted that there is a tendency on the part of some Catholics to be selective in their adherence to the Church's moral teachings. It is sometimes claimed that dissent from the magisterium is totally compatible with being a "good Catholic" and poses no obstacle to the reception of the sacraments. This is a grave error that challenges the teaching office of the bishops of the United States and elsewhere.[7]

What, then, is the status of those "cafeteria Catholics"?

I hope this lengthy discussion has clearly indicated that Mr. Fitzgerald's initial question about marginal Catholics was a very good one, that it surfaced many other challenging inquiries, and that making judgments about the faith level of another person is indeed risky. Its complexity may be the main reason why Catholic Church authorities move cautiously and slowly against members who disagree with some of its tenets or disobey its regulations.

Slow and Cautious Church Reactions

A Canadian author has noted this caution and reluctance. Anne Roche Muggeridge, in *The Desolate City*, maintains that the Catholic Church has suffered an inner revolution since around 1960. She contends that the Catholic hierarchical concept, the belief that moral authority derives from God and is exercised in the Church by direct commission from Christ and through the apostolic succession, has been under attack especially by liberal theologians. They wish, in her opinion, to replace that notion with a basically Protestant principle of authority which is anti-dogmatic and anti-hierarchical, which glorifies private judgment and which caters to the rebellious "I will not serve" attitude described in Genesis following the original fall.[8]

While Muggeridge would approve of the Church correcting theologians like Hans Küng and Charles Curran more firmly and swiftly, she recognizes that historically it has never done so. "Rome is almost pitifully eager to accept a plausible explanation; it is, in spite of what its critics say, extremely reluctant to separate even the most reprobate from communion with the Church. The Church never forgets its chief responsibility: to save sinners, not to cast them into outer darkness."[9]

We can see that demonstrated in quite opposite circumstances — the cases of Archbishop Lefebvre and Father Curran.

* After a series of exchanges initiated by Pope John Paul II between Vatican officials and Archbishop Marcel Lefebvre, a document or protocol note was signed by Cardinal Ratzinger and the archbishop on May 5, 1988, outlining steps for a reconciliation of his St. Pius X Society with the Apostolic See. In summary, the archbishop and members of his Society agreed to accept the teaching authority of the Church and to regard the reforms of the Second Vatican Council as legitimate; in return, the Society would be able to use pre-Vatican II liturgical rites, enjoy a special status in the Roman Catholic Church and have a person from within its ranks ordained a bishop.[10]

For some reason, the very next day Archbishop Lefebvre changed his mind. Shortly thereafter he wrote to Pope John Paul II reiterating his objections to developments in the Church since Vatican II. Moreover, he intimated his intentions of moving ahead, without the pope's permission, to ordain several members of the St. Pius X Society as bishops.[11]

Despite rejection of his conciliatory attempts, Pope John Paul II responded with an earnest plea for Lefebvre to abandon plans to ordain bishops without papal permission. That step would violate canons 1013 and 1382 of Church law and incur automatic excommunication from the Church for him and the bishops being consecrated. He wrote:

> It is with heartfelt and deep pain that I take note of your letter.... With a paternal heart... I exhort you, venerable brother, to give up your project.... I ardently invite you to return, in humility, to full obedience to the vicar of

Christ.... I ask it of you in the name of the wounds of
Christ... who on the eve of his passion prayed for his disciples, "so that they may all be one" (John 17:21).... Dear
brother, do not permit this year dedicated in a special way
to God's mother to bring yet another wound to her
mother's heart![12]

As a further effort to bring about reconciliation and stave off
schism, the Pope sent a personal car to Econe, Switzerland, the night
before the unauthorized ordination, asking Lefebvre and the four
priests designated for the episcopacy to come to Rome. The archbishop refused and went ahead with the ceremony.

But despite this action which brought excommunication, the
Church while warning followers that they would be excommunicated if they stayed with the rebel prelate, promised to meet their
traditionalist needs if they remained loyal to the papacy. Moreover,
even the canons which prohibit excommunicated persons from receiving the sacraments of the Catholic Church make no judgments
about the individuals involved as to their faith level, the status of
their souls or their prospects for eternal salvation.

* The Church also took a similar slow and cautious approach
to moral theologian Father Charles Curran and his teachings on
divorce and remarriage, abortion, euthanasia, masturbation, premarital intercourse and homosexual acts. Investigations of his writ-
ings apparently were underway from 1966, and he was informed
officially on August 2, 1979, that the Vatican Congregation for the
Doctrine of the Faith was studying his positions on these matters.[13]

It requires an entire book to describe, or at least sketch, the
written and personal, private and public exchanges between the
Vatican and Curran over almost a decade following that initial contact in the summer of 1979. Only on July 25, 1986, did Cardinal
Joseph Ratzinger write:

In light of your repeated refusal to accept what the Church
teaches and in light of its mandate to promote and safeguard the Church's teaching on faith and morals through-

out the Catholic world, this Congregation, in agreement with the Congregation for Catholic Education, sees no alternative now but to advise the Most Reverend Chancellor that you will no longer be considered suitable nor eligible to exercise the function of a Professor of Catholic Theology.[14]

The communication also noted that Pope John Paul II approved both the content of the letter and the procedure followed.

However painful this well-publicized action by Rome, the last paragraph of Ratzinger's letter still reiterated the Church's desire for reconciliation: "May I finally express the sincere hope that this regrettable, but necessary, outcome to the Congregation's study might move you to reconsider your dissenting positions and to accept in its fullness the teaching of the Catholic Church."[15] Moreover, the moral theologian was not suspended as a priest. In fact, his own bishop stated that the decision did not affect Father Curran's good standing as a priest of the Diocese of Rochester, "where he will always be welcome to exercise his priestly ministry."

As with Archbishop Lefebvre, there was no mention or judgment about Father Curran's faith, the status of his soul or the prospects of his eternal salvation.

There are, of course, many obvious differences between the situations of Archbishop Lefebvre and Father Curran. Moreover, some commentators, in the United States particularly, feel very strongly that the moral theologian was not extended as much respect, love and personal contact as was given the recalcitrant prelate. In their judgment, the tone of exchanges differed.

The point of the comparisons between the two cases in this book, however, is simply to demonstrate that in both circumstances the Church moved slowly and cautiously. Such slowness and caution was based, at least in part, upon a recognition of the difficulty or almost impossibility of matching external criteria with inner faith and spiritual status with surface behavior. In addition, the Church in both instances seemed anxious to give the person involved the benefit of the doubt and explicitly expressed hopes and openness for an eventual change of heart and reconciliation.

The Church takes a similar cautious approach to the more immediate matter of this book — baptism and marriage. It demands that the person(s) seeking either of these sacraments must have faith, for the sacraments are "sacraments of faith" and "presuppose faith,"[16] but, as we will discuss in later chapters, its regulations about the faith of recipients require a minimal level of belief and are far less restrictive than the policies and practices in some parishes or areas of our country.

Marginal Catholics: A Working Definition

Now, finally, as promised, we give our definition of marginal Catholics. In the following pages, by "marginal Catholics" we mean those who have only a tenuous link with the parish. This fragile bond is manifested when persons seeking a sacrament either do not participate weekly at Sunday Mass, or seldom receive communion and penance, or rarely volunteer for church activities, or never formally register with a particular parish. The presence of any one of those negative characteristics is sufficient, for the purposes of our discussion, to place these people in the marginal Catholic category.

There are, naturally, degrees of marginalization. The case of the person who has not been to church in ten years differs greatly from that of the individual who goes regularly to Mass, but chooses not to affiliate or become involved with any parish. The challenge presented by the latter to the priest, deacon or pastoral leader is rather minimal; the challenge offered by the former is quite substantial.

Whenever a Catholic requests one of the Church's sacraments, there is always a need for that person to be challenged. As we will see in the next chapter, the lifelong Christian journey involves a series of large and small conversions or turning points. Jesus constantly summons us to change our lives and believe in the gospel.

That call to reform, to make a fresh start and to move forward happens daily, but occurs in a unique way at the time of sacramental encounters. If such challenges are therefore necessary for every mainstream Catholic, then obviously they are even more critical for marginal ones.

When pastoral leaders challenge these so-called inactive, non-practicing, fallen away or "bad" Catholics, however, they must do it with great caution. They do not want to crush those who have displayed some signs of good will and faith by their very request for baptism, matrimony or another of the sacraments. They also must be careful not to slip into the judgment-making we have discussed. Our working definition of marginal Catholics is merely an elemental and surface delineation based on several external criteria. Caution, consequently, will keep us from making automatic assumptions about the non-existence or low level of faith and adherence to the Church.

This caution will, finally, lead our challenging of the marginal Catholic to follow an extremely personal and highly individualized approach, for reasons we will now explore.

Guidance from the *Catechism*

Article 754: "The Church is… the flock of which God himself foretold that he would be the shepherd, and whose sheep, even though governed by human shepherds, are unfailingly nourished and led by Christ himself, the Good Shepherd and Prince of Shepherds, who gave his life for his sheep" (*LG* 6; cf. *Jn* 10:1-10; *Isa* 40:11; *Ezek* 34:11-31; *Jn* 10:11; *1 Pet* 5:4; *Jn* 10:11-16).

Article 820: "Christ always gives his Church the gift of unity, but the Church must always pray and work to maintain, reinforce, and perfect the unity that Christ wills for her" (cf. *Jn* 17:21; *Heb* 7:25).

Article 825: In the Church's "members perfect holiness is something yet to be acquired…" (cf. *LG* 11 §3).

Article 827: The Church, "clasping sinners to her bosom, at once holy and always in need of purification, follows constantly the path of penance and renewal (*LG* 8 §3; cf. *UR* 3; *Heb* 2:17; 7:26; *2 Cor* 5:21). All members of the Church, including her ministers, must acknowledge that they are sinners" (cf. *1 Jn* 1:8-10).

2 The Process Called Conversion

I was raised in a non-practicing Lutheran family. Bill was raised in a practicing Catholic family, practicing in the sense that they went to church every Sunday and holy day. But in his family you went to church because you were *supposed* to and for no other reason. He had sat in the back pew his entire life and had never actually understood what was going on. He was never taught a love for the Church, a respect for the beautiful tradition, or even an understanding of the magnificent prayer we call Mass. He was taught nothing except you go because we say so. When we became engaged I became Catholic through six weeks of hurried instruction when all that was really on my mind was marrying the man I loved. Serious obligation to Church or future family was not a priority at that time. We had a beautiful Nuptial Mass, moved to a city 180 miles away, and immediately proceeded to stop going to church. If you look at our backgrounds, you can understand why neither of us found attendance at church of any importance. Add to that the fact we were young and foolish and in love. We didn't so much leave the Church as we simply ignored it.

We moved back home to our small town and when our first child was born, it was very important to both of us to have her baptized. Even though we didn't go to church, we still loved God and felt an obligation to baptize this child he had sent us. The priest was the same one who had married us and he gladly baptized our baby. He may have said something about our obligation to attend church, I honestly don't remember, but I do know he did nothing to alienate us. We, again, didn't attend church, but when our daughter turned six and was old enough to go to religious education classes, we sent her because we loved God and wanted her to learn about God. And we now attended church occasionally, especially when the children were involved in something special.

The following year we had our second child, who was premature and in immediate danger of death. I called the church and asked for the priest to come and baptize her. I was told he was out of town. No one came, I did not even know that a lay person could baptize, so nothing was done. As they sent my newborn daughter 200 miles away on "Flight for Life," all I could do was pray that God would watch over her. No one from the church ever came. For weeks we prayed alone and sat by our baby's bedside. God did watch over our little girl and answered our prayers even though we didn't regularly attend church, as she lived to become a perfectly normal and healthy child. When the crisis had passed and we got our baby home, there was some hurt in us that the Church hadn't been there for us when we needed it, but still no alienation of any sort. When the hurt died down, we again approached the Church to baptize our baby. This time it was a different priest. I do remember much more of a lecture about regular attendance at church, but he still agreed to baptize her, and again we were not driven away.

Two more years passed without us attending church. Although I can say I do remember *many* conversations about us going. We knew we should, and were feeling a very strong pull to the Church, but we did not go at that time. Then our church acquired a new priest who felt very strongly about calling home non-practicing Catholics. A group of the young families from the church sponsored a hayride and barbecue for marginal Catholics. We were invited and accepted. No one said anything about our coming to church; they just made us feel welcome to be among them. We have not missed a Sunday or holy day Mass since the night of that barbecue!

That was four and a half years ago. In that time I have served as a CCD instructor, sewn all new linens for the altar and decorated the sanctuary for Masses. My husband is right now the president of our Pastoral Council and the Grand Knight of our Knights of Columbus council. Our oldest daughter is in preparation for First Holy Communion. We all *love* our church, and we go and we participate because we love it, not because *we have* to. My husband and I have both attended many different class situations and have done lots of independent reading to learn all we can about this Church we love so dearly.

I know I've made this long, but it seemed like the only way to tell our story. My point is, I think we are worthwhile to the Church and I don't know if things would have turned out this way if a priest had turned us away from the Church at any time. Maybe we were lucky in that we dealt with priests who allowed us to develop at our own pace. We never lacked a love for God, only a way of serving him. When I read stories of people being denied having their children baptized, it scares me because maybe they are the Church of tomorrow (the CCD teachers, or lectors, or Pastoral Council presidents), but they've been given no reason to feel wanted back. Maybe they leave feeling it is no longer their Church after all; it just turned them away! It seems to me the Church should accept people at whatever level of faith they are, and give them reason to build and grow.   — *Colorado*

David O'Rourke was a senior at Yale during the 1950's and destined for Columbia Law School after graduation when an unusual experience turned his life around. Some Catholic friends invited him to spend the weekend with them on retreat at a New England Trappist monastery. He had never made a retreat before and had never seen a monastery, but nevertheless decided to go along with his colleagues.

Observing these monks who really believed what they were doing, who followed a pattern of prayer, silence, manual labor and asceticism proved "unsettling" to him and his friends. For O'Rourke it became a significant step in the major conversion of his life. The Trappist weekend coupled with several other incidents led him to cancel plans for Columbia, to spend the next year studying scholastic philosophy at a Dominican House of Studies in France, and eventually to become a priest himself.[1]

Meaning of Conversion

Reflection on his own experiences and upon several decades of priestly ministry, has brought him to the conclusion that such conversions or turning points in peoples' lives are not magic moments, but human processes. They include occasions and characteristics we can understand. They may occur in an instant or over a long period. They normally are more complex and more involved than a simple event or a moment in time. They involve duration and continuity. They involve not only an event, or a number of isolated events, but a series of related events played out over a span of months or even years. They involve not only the events, but the people in the events, and all that they go through as they experience the events described. They involve time, change and growth.[2]

The lengthy letter from Colorado which began this chapter exemplifies, through the lives of that couple and family, all those abstract statements in very concrete ways.

Use of the word "conversion" however, may confuse some. That term traditionally has referred to "converts," to persons who previously possessed no religion at all or belonged to a different religious tradition and decided, under God's grace, to enter the Roman Catholic Church. Conversion today does not exclude that particular understanding, but embraces a wider set of personal "turning." It connotes any process of moving from one attitude or status to another.

In the setting of this book, conversion can denote the turning from no religion to some religion, from no belief to some belief, from a sinful, destructive way of life to a virtuous, constructive manner of living, from being an inactive Catholic to becoming an active one, from routinely carrying out one's religious duties to doing so with fire-like fervor, from leading a good life to leading an even better one.

A Personal Process

There are two key words in this conversion or turning experience as applied to sacramental encounters in general and baptism or marriage in particular: personal and process. Each conversion is, or at least should be, totally personal, unique, individual. Each case is different, every person follows a singular journey. Moreover, each conversion entails a process which takes time and travels an uneven, not always direct or ever-forward path.

These personal and process components of conversion require both respect and patience from those in pastoral ministry. They need to respect the Holy Spirit's gentle, often surprising and hidden movement within the hearts of people. In addition, they need to wait with patience, understanding that journeys of faith move at their own frequently slow pace and usually cannot be hurried.

The author of our introductory letter underscored that point. The note concluded by observing that she and her husband needed a long time to learn how to love and serve God.

Support for Patience and Respect

Several contemporary Church phenomena provide sound theological and pastoral support for a respectful and patience-filled approach to the sacraments. We will examine those now and add illustrations to demonstrate their application to our concerns in this book.

1. *The Rite of Christian Initiation of Adults*[3]

Various sections of the introduction to this ritual speak about the conversion, journey, gradual process and growth elements of Christian initiation.

The rite has been designed "for adults who, after hearing the mystery of Christ proclaimed, consciously and freely seek the living God and enter the way of faith and conversion as the Holy Spirit opens their hearts. By God's help they will be strengthened spiritually during their preparation and at the proper time will receive the sacraments fruitfully (no. 1)."

This is a "gradual process that takes place within the community of the faithful. By joining the catechumens in reflecting on the value of the Paschal Mystery and by renewing their own conversion, the faithful provide an example that will help the catechumens to obey the Holy Spirit more generously (no. 4)."

The spiritual journey of adults "varies according to the many forms of God's grace, the free cooperation of the individuals, the action of the Church and the circumstances of time and place (no. 5)."

This itinerary includes "periods for making inquiry and for maturing," for progression in faith, "for deepening the Christian experience, for spiritual growth, and for entering more fully into the life and unity of the community (nos. 6-7)."

The diverse and flexible rites for Christian Initiation naturally reflect the ritual's stated awareness of the variable and unique nature of this conversion process.

Two Examples

The New Catholics contains the stories of 17 contemporary persons who experienced such a conversion and have entered the Church.[4] These include several best-selling authors, well-known university professors, a peace activist, a former Protestant missionary, an entertainer, a former Episcopal priest, a rock star turned Franciscan friar, an ex-Buddhist, a feminist, a political scientist, a one-time radical and others.

They share certain common traits: a great respect for Pope John Paul II and the magisterium, a strong love for the sacramental life of the Church, especially the Eucharist, and a deep commitment to social justice. They also mirror the myriad paths or journeys which people follow in the conversion process.

John Cort was one. He worked as a reporter, editor, union organizer, Peace Corps and antipoverty official, free-lance writer and co-editor of a journal, *Religious Socialism.* An honors graduate in 1935 from Harvard University, he became a Catholic while an undergraduate student at that Ivy League school.

Many factors influenced him along his own conversion path — university professors, serious study of philosophical and theological questions, an unrequited love and even the opposition of his father. After Cort began instructions, his father, son of a frontier missionary for the Reformed Church in Iowa, wrote an angry letter to the dean of Harvard complaining about his son's Catholic-leaning tutor. He also informed his own son that if he insisted on being received into the Church, he would insist on withdrawing him from Harvard. Cort relates what happened:

> This rather appealed to my sense of melodrama, but I felt I should at least inform Father Greene. He in turn asked the pastor, a Monsignor Hickey, for guidance and Monsignor Hickey advised me to wait until after graduation. Being then much more receptive to the counsel of monsignori than I have since become, I agreed and did not

officially become a Catholic until after graduation in June
of 1935, when I was received at the altar of a church on
Pineapple Street in Brooklyn Heights. My witnesses were
the housekeeper and the sexton, who put down his broom
for a few minutes to stand beside me.[5]

In later life he thanked God for those different influences
which led him to the Church and for how very happy he had been
in it. He regretted that "some of my fellow Catholics — lay and
cleric — seem to be losing their faith in the magisterium of the
Church and in those ancient truths of the Gospel that the magisterium upholds. I keep telling them, 'I've been where you are head-
ing and, believe me, you wouldn't like it.'"[6]

Judy Valentine Gerth graduated from Michigan State in 1959
and eventually became executive director of the Catholic Church
Extension Society in Chicago. Her entrance into the Church just
prior to Vatican II likewise illustrates a conversion's crooked road
filled with potholes and detours.

The experience of kneeling and praying in church was new
to me. The chapel was old, dark, and musty and there were
numerous statues and candles. Just being there was com-
forting. I focused my thoughts and carefully repeated
newly learned prayers and devotions like the Hail Mary
and the Stations of the Cross. I soaked up Catholicism in
that quiet chapel.

When I returned to college in the fall, a Catholic
friend regularly accompanied me to early morning Mass
on campus. Knowing she could have used the extra sleep,
I was impressed by her devotion to her friend and her faith.
Even though I could not participate fully in the Mass, I
still felt at home. I was amazed that so many other students
got up so early to attend daily Mass. I had to believe something was going on for them, too.

Then came a doubtful, dry period. Nothing appeared
to be falling into place. I felt I was making no progress in

my spiritual life. I examined Eastern religions, Judaism, and, disheartened, even considered agnosticism. The enthusiasm I felt the year before seemed to have evaporated. I was confused because I thought I should feel more definite, more convinced that Catholicism was "the answer." Without the assurance, I lapsed into spiritual apathy. A persistence within me, however, would not go away.

I tried again. I took the catechism course for the second time, and although the priest pronounced me ready, I remained hesitant, a state of indecision that continued for weeks. I felt spiritually stuck — I simply could not move. But I did not forget to pray.

One day as I knelt at the altar the following words came to me: what are you waiting for? Go ahead. I stood up and felt the doubt slip away. I was ready.[7]

However, Judy Gerth's up and down spiritual journey continued afterwards. "I wish I could say my faith life was changed at that moment. I wish I could say that my First Communion and confirmation had the spiritual highs I expected them to have, but it wasn't so. My conversion was not the end of my pilgrimage. It was only the beginning."[8]

Her faith needed growth and development. With this example in mind, we move to the next point.

2. *Development of Faith*

During the past several decades great attention has been given by philosophers and psychologists to the growth and development of the human person. The names of Erik H. Erikson, Daniel J. Levinson, Carol Gilligan and Lawrence Kohlberg stand out, among others, as pioneers in the field. They have studied and theorized about the ages and seasons of a person's life and have also researched and conjectured about female and male development.

James W. Fowler, professor of theology and human development at Atlanta's Emory University, has with his associates complemented those studies with research and theories on faith development. They have identified seven stages of faith: primal, intuitive-projective, mythic-literal, synthetic-conventional, individuative-reflective, conjunctive and universalizing.[9]

At the risk of oversimplification, we could state, based on their studies and concepts, that there are different kinds, stages or levels of faith in an infant, a two-year-old, an elementary school age child, an adolescent, a young adult, a mid-life person and a person who has "aged to perfection."

Fowler cautions, however, that the crucial point of the faith development theory is not that human completion or wholeness is "an estate to be attained or a stage to be realized." Instead, "it is a way of being and moving, a way of being on pilgrimage." The goal is "not for everyone to reach the stage of universalizing faith. Rather, it is for each person or group to open themselves, as radically as possible — within the structures of their present stage or transition — to synergy with Spirit."[10]

Two Examples

The Colorado couple illustrate this faith development theory lived out in reality. Bill's stage of belief motivated him to move from regular, but back pew attendance at Mass, to non-attendance, to sporadic appearances in church and ultimately to weekly participation in the Eucharist and active involvement in the life of the parish. His wife's pilgrimage of faith led her to enter the Church for mixed motives, to only occasional Mass participation, and eventually to consistent attendance at Sunday Eucharist, active engagement in parish life, and admirable efforts in building belief within the youth of that area, her children included.

Peace activist Jim Forest entered the Church in 1960. His journey to Catholicism was circuitous like most others and, similarly, his pilgrimage as a Catholic after baptism likewise has been an uneven adventure. In his words:

"Would you do it again?" a student asked me more than a decade later when I was teaching a theology class at a college. She had been born and raised a Catholic, felt estranged from the Church, and could not imagine anyone actually joining it.

Yes, I said. Yes, and yet again, yes. But I assured her it had not been easy for me. In the years since coming into the Church, I had several times tried to give it up, generally because of brokenness and failure in my own life, or disappointment and anger with various people in the hierarchy, or some mixture of both. But I found it was impossible to get along without the Eucharist. I became homesick for Mass and never could manage more than a few weeks without it. But in those hungry weeks I managed to become a bit more compassionate about both bishops and myself (or myself and even bishops), and hopeful that God hadn't given up on any of us. I also learned, crisis by crisis, that I could no more renounce the Catholic Church than abandon my parents.[11]

3. *The Stages of Grief*

Dr. Elisabeth Kübler-Ross, in her classic reference work *On Death and Dying,* outlined the stages that deathly sick persons generally pass through in their last weeks, days and hours.[12] Denial, anger, bargaining, sadness and acceptance are familiar terms for people working today in the pastoral ministry field. We also understand that those stages likewise hold true for people who care for, or about, dying individuals. Counselors also now recognize that others who have suffered a deep personal loss such as a divorce, job transfer, dismissal from work or death of a dream may experience corresponding sentiments.

In all these situations, however, the stages of grief are neither chronological or stable, nor always present. They are not mechanical or mathematical. People do not necessarily move from the first through each to the last. They are not comparable to courses leading to academic graduation which must be passed successfully to secure the desired degree (acceptance). Persons may go back and forth, in and out of different stages, and encounter all five within an hour's time. Some individuals skip one stage or another, or never move beyond denial and never reach an attitude of acceptance.

It seems to me there is a distinct parallel between the stages of grief according to the Kübler-Ross analysis and the stages of faith observed by many pastoral ministers.

Some persons never move beyond the faith of a child or youngster; others grow gradually and arrive at a very mature faith level; still others, like our Colorado couple, practice the faith, then let it lie dormant, then through various events leap forward to a new stage in the faith development.

Priest confessors can testify to this perhaps better than anyone else, particularly at special moments of reconciliation like Christmas or Easter. Penitents away for years from the Church, Mass and communion, approach the sacraments. What brought them to this new awareness and fresh rediscovery of their faith? It may be the death of one they love, the approaching First Communion of a child, a major moral lapse which jolted their inner state, a bitter disappointment, or the boredom of mid-life. For some, there is no such major event or circumstance, but rather a gradual stirring of the heart. Those Spirit-given impulses frequently will bring the person back to Sunday Mass for several months, or even years, before taking that additional measure of confession or reconciliation.

The phases of believing and practicing one's beliefs thus often may alternate between moving ahead and slipping behind, between being apparently at one moment on fire with faith and at another time wearied or bored by the whole spiritual struggle. The challenge for pastoral leaders in the Church is to "accept people at whatever level of faith they are, and give them reason to build and grow."

An Example

Some people, according to Jimmy Breslin, will come back to God and rediscover their faith when they get a chest pain. But for Maura Moynihan it was the experience of a different religion, in a different culture, in a different country which reawakened her faith and religious involvement.

To set the scene, here is how she described herself:

> I've just returned from a year in India where I was working for the Smithsonian. Prior to that I worked as a journalist at the *New York Post* and *Interview,* and I'm freelancing now for *Vogue, American Heritage,* and the *New Republic.* I'm also an actress and singer and I have a band. I've been in five movies and several plays and television series like *The New Show;* I gave that up temporarily because it just wasn't satisfying enough, but now I'm back at it. I'm planning to do a children's book on Hindu and Buddhist myths. I'm also very active in politics and am toying with the idea of pursuing politics as a career. I guess you could say I'm at a crossroads in my life.[13]

Her father goes to church all the time, but her mother had a terrible reaction against religion and Catholicism. Ms. Moynihan moved to India at 15 when her father was appointed ambassador there. During the years which followed, she both lost a sense of belonging to the Catholic Church, and yet found in India her faith and involvement in religion reawakened. Much later, poor financially and spiritually, and working her way around Paris by odd jobs like singing at sidewalk cafes and doing street theater, she entered the Notre Dame Cathedral and had an "overwhelming feeling of faith."

> I burst into tears and felt a reawakening of faith that had not happened to me for a very long time. I used to go to church to feel close to God, but didn't feel that *personal*

ecstasy that I felt at Hindu temples. But this day I decided
that it was my dharma to be a Catholic — after all, why
was I *born* a Catholic? But I decided that I was not going
to reject Hinduism. I was just going to incorporate what
I'd learned. To me, Hinduism still had a lot of answers that
I wasn't getting from Christianity, from a priest, from
Catholic friends, or from going to Mass on Sunday.[14]

She summarized her own spiritual pilgrimage in this way:

I think that my going away from the Church for those years
and immersing myself in an entirely different tradition has
made me come back to it with entirely fresh eyes. I'm not
just going through the rote motions because I learned them
as a child. I came to it entirely of my own volition and my
own longing, without any kind of judgment — consider-
ing myself a Hindu, not thinking of myself as a Catholic
— and have rediscovered how wonderful the Catholic service is and how much it is trying to instill love, forgiveness,
and brotherhood. I know it sounds corny and prosaic to
say things like that, but good God, that's what the human
race needs, isn't it? Still, I think that the Church isn't doing enough to bring back young people who have lapsed.

I would like to reinvolve people in faith because it
means so much to me, especially in the nuclear era. If I
didn't have faith, I don't think I would be able to get up
in the morning, I don't think I'd be able to live.[15]

4. *Signs of the Times*

Some sociologists hold that in contemporary society many,
perhaps most young people become alienated from all social institutions, including the Church, in their late teens and do not rees-
tablish a positive relationship with them until the end of their twenties.[16]

Statistical research tends to confirm that assertion.

One project studied the percentage of young people who attend Mass almost every week according to their age level. The table below summarizes results of the analysis.[17]

Age	Attendance at Mass
13-17	67%
18-22	49%
23-27	29%
28-30	32%

The same study finds, as might be expected, a similar pattern among young people who receive communion almost every week.[18]

Age	Communion Almost Every Week
13-17	54%
18-22	32%
23-27	17%
28-30	21%

A more recent analysis reflects the same trends for Catholics in 1985.[19]

Age	Attended Church in Past 7 Days
Teens	64%
18-23	36%
25-29	39%
30-49	54%
50-64	64%
Over 65	71%

Such data about the times in which we live should temper our pastoral approach to those in early age levels who seek certain sacraments.

Confirmation

Confirmation is a case in point. The controversy continues over the appropriate age for this sacrament. Should it be a complement to baptism and be received prior to the Eucharist (the liturgists' argument based on ancient patristic studies) or be an adult commitment rite and be delayed until late teens (the religious educators' argument based on contemporary psychological theories)? Those parish leaders who espouse the latter practice, probably a majority in the United States today, often stress to candidates that this is the occasion for them to make an adult, permanent commitment to Jesus Christ. While that obviously is a beautiful ideal to propose, one could question the wisdom of such emphasis for teenagers. These adolescents are hardly able to sustain any type of commitment, are about to or are already entering an anti-institutional stage of their lives, and in many instances, as statistics reveal, will probably abandon regular practice of the faith from the late teens until the late twenties.

A better approach theologically, as we will discuss in a future chapter, and pastorally, based on these statistical surveys, might instead follow this path. Parish instructors could underscore the teenagers' growing maturity and ability to appreciate sacramental encounters. In addition, they might explain for them the God-given power of the sacrament of confirmation to convey wisdom and strength for their ongoing Christian journey over the years ahead.

Turning Times and Pastoral Approaches

My own experiences and many conversations with clergy, here and in Canada, indicate that major conversions in terms of returning to full, active participation in the life of the Church *do not* come for most couples at their wedding or the baptism of their first child (children). While those occasions, handled well pastorally, can keep alive their flickering faith and perhaps enkindle it a bit, the major turning generally occurs when the initial youngster nears the age, even remotely, for First Communion. That frequently coincides with the parents' arrival at their late twenties and early thirties — statistically proven times for a return to earlier faith values and practices.

The content and thrust of this chapter should not be interpreted as encouraging a pessimistic, fatalistic attitude toward those who seek baptism or marriage. Neither does it intend to discourage or minimize the excellent and well-established instructive preparation programs in existence for both. The concepts we have presented, if anything, highlight the importance of all these efforts which challenge people to be more, which portray the rich meaning of each sacrament and which enunciate clearly all the consequent responsibilities flowing out of a baptismal or matrimonial encounter with Christ.

Our presentation, however, may shift the *how* not the *what* of preparation endeavors and could alter, not the religious ideal conveyed, but the pastoral leaders' expectations.

Following a discussion of these notions about the conversion process, a priest participant at a clergy institute on baptism and marriage commented: "I always considered these as times for catechesis; now I view them as occasions for evangelization."

Those who ask for baptism or marriage are in the midst of long spiritual journeys following pilgrimage paths which are highly personalized, uneven and mysterious. This calls for gentle patience and awesome respect upon the part of Church personnel working with couples about to marry and parents seeking to baptize their child. These leaders indeed are evangelists at those sensitive moments.

Sacred Scripture, old and new, offers us guidance and support, instruction and models as we continue our study of the best ways for reaching out to marginal Catholics.

Guidance from the *Catechism*

Article 1426: "…the new life received in Christian initiation has not abolished the frailty and weakness of human nature, nor the inclination to sin that tradition calls *concupiscence*, which remains in the baptized such that with the help of the grace of Christ they may prove themselves in the struggle of Christian life (cf. Council of Trent (1546): DS 1515). This is the struggle of *conversion* directed toward holiness and eternal life to which the Lord never ceases to call us (cf. Council of Trent (1547): DS 1545; *LG* 40)."

Article 1430: "Jesus' call to conversion… does not aim first at outward works… but at the *conversion of the heart, interior conversion.*"

Article 1431: "Interior repentance is a radical reorientation of our whole life, a return, a conversion to God with all our heart, an end of sin, a turning away from evil…. At the same time it entails the desire and resolution to change one's life with hope in God's mercy and trust in the help of his grace."

Article 1435: "Conversion is accomplished in daily life by gestures of reconciliation, concern for the poor, the exercise and defense of justice and right, (cf. *Am* 5:24; *Isa* 1:17) by the admission of faults… revision of life, examination of conscience, spiritual direction, acceptance of suffering, endurance of persecution for the sake of righteousness."

3 A Biblical Perspective

I have experienced both sides of the fence, and have been both helped and hurt by the clergy.

My first experience was positive. After many years of having been out of the Church, a Catholic priest in the Navy asked to talk with me. He listened to my story, gave me confession, and invited me back into the Church. I could not turn him down because of the way he approached me. It was non-judgmental, patient and with compassion. He did not try to sell me anything. He just said, "God loves you so much that he allowed his son to die for you. He doesn't hold grudges; He only forgives those in need. His son Jesus did not come here for the people who followed God's laws, but for those who did not, those who had normal, human defects of character." So I came back, and have not left, despite the negative experience.

My negative experience was when I desired to get married. I was in the Navy and was marrying a person from another country. The immigration law said we must be married within 90 days; the Catholic Church said you cannot be married for six months. So we got married by a judge. Then I was stationed in Bremerton, Washington. The priest at our parish told us to go to the priest on board my ship. I was on a nuclear ship; my fiancee was not a citizen and therefore could not come onboard the ship to see the priest. So the priest told me to use the priest at the naval station. That priest told me to go to my parish priest. So after coming full circle, I went through the routine a second time and gave up. I felt they were lazy or did not want my business. I could not receive the sacraments, but we continued to attend Mass.

I must explain that my case was more complicated than I may have led you to believe. I had been previously married, again by a civil servant — a city mayor. I was divorced by civil law. We never married in the Church. So, we needed an annulment. The point, however, was that no one would tell us what we had to do. Another positive. We were transferred to San Diego for duty. There we went to Mass every Sunday. One of the priests asked why we never received communion, so we told him the above story. He invited us into his office and explained what we had to do for an annulment and to be married in the Church. We followed his direction and were married in the Church on our fifth wedding anniversary. That was over three years ago.

We are now active in the Church. My wife sings in the choir and is a member of the Women's Guild. I belong to the Knights of Columbus, serve as a liturgical minister, and am in our diocesan education program sponsored by the Bishop, which is a two year program of faith sharing and didactic studies. This will allow us to go further if we desire and my thoughts at the present time lean to the diaconate.   — *California*

Scripture scholar Father Raymond E. Brown, in discussing the roles of women in the fourth gospel, mentions an approach for this type of study: to examine specific texts referring either to the equality or the subordination of women in society and cult. He is not convinced, however, of the usefulness of such a procedure, "since for every text pointing in one direction there is usually a counter-text."[1]

In Ephesians, for example, we read that wives must be subject in everything to their husbands; however, this entire section on the relationship between spouses is introduced by the verse which commands, "Defer to one another out of reverence for Christ" (Eph 5:24; 21). One text seems to counter the other.

We must express similar reservations about citing biblical texts to support a particular pastoral approach with regard to marginal Catholics.

Those who establish or advocate strict and rigidly enforced rules about regular Mass attendance and active Church involvement as requisites for the sacrament of baptism or matrimony might quote the book of Revelation's strong rebuke to lukewarm members. To the church in Laodicea, the author was instructed to write: "I know your works; I know that you are neither cold nor hot. I wish you were either cold or hot. So, because you are lukewarm, neither hot nor cold, I will spit you out of my mouth" (Rv 3:15-16).

Or they could point to Jesus' warning, "Whoever is not with me is against me, and whoever does not gather with me scatters" (Mt 12:30).

Or, again, they might stress the Savior's teaching that the greatest commandments are to love God and neighbor with "all your heart, with all your soul, with all your mind, and with all your strength" (Mk 12:29-33).

On the other hand, those who follow or advocate a more flexible policy might look to Christ's parable about the weeds among the wheat. Do not pull up the weeds, Jesus said, because you "might uproot the wheat along with them. Let them grow together until harvest…" (Mt 13:24).

Or they could point to the image of the Good Shepherd in the gospels who is always seeking out the lost or strayed (Lk 15:1-7; Mt 18:12-14; Mt 10:6, 15:24; Jn 10).

Or, again, they might stress the Lucan parables about the lost sheep, coin or son (Lk 15).

For this reason, we entitled the present chapter *a* not *the* biblical perspective. With the assistance of some scripture scholars, I will simply explore what kind of directions the Old and New Tes-

tament give us for responding to marginal Catholics.[2] Others surely
can discover patterns in the Bible different from those sketched
below. The following, however, have a sound base and are helpful
to me.

Old Testament

• *A jealous God.* The first testament, the Hebrew scriptures,
portrays a God who seemingly does not tolerate marginal followers or lukewarm believers. Yahweh is "a jealous God" who demands
the kind of exclusive allegiance which a spouse must have for a
spouse.[3] That Jewish insistence on strict loyalty to the one God grew
out of a desire to distinguish Israel from her Near Eastern neighbors, all of whom worshiped a host of heavenly deities.[4]

"You shall not worship any other god, for the Lord is the Jealous One; a Jealous God is he" (Ex 34:14). So great was the danger
of the chosen people being corrupted, absorbed or compromised
by surrounding inhabitants that they were to make no agreements
with them, destroy signs of their false worship and never inter-
marry.[5]

"For the Lord, your God, is a consuming fire, a jealous God"
(Dt 4:24). Yahweh alone is God, a God who is one and holy; Israel
must realize that it can serve no other.[6]

"For the Lord, your God, who is in your midst, is a jealous
God" (Dt 6:15). Yahweh is the master of nature and history, a holy,
living God, the one who gives rain and the increase in the world
around us. This personal, jealous God is not a force of nature to be
appeased by magical rites.[7]

• *Slow to anger, rich in kindness.* That jealous God, however,
while never allowing marginal loyalty, still always welcomes home
those who sincerely repent of their infidelity. "The Lord, the Lord,
a merciful and gracious God, slow to anger and rich in kindness and
fidelity..." (Ex 34:7).

"The Lord is slow to anger and rich in kindness, forgiving

wickedness and crime…" (Nb 14:18). "Slow to anger" or "patient" is contrasted with "quick-tempered" in Proverbs 14:29.

The prophet Joel, urging the people of Israel to undergo a true conversion, reminds them of Yahweh's parental compassion and kindness — qualities or characteristics proclaimed earlier in Exodus. This God is voluntarily and perpetually committed to Israel's welfare (Ex 34:7).

> Rend your hearts, not your garments,
>   and return to the Lord, your God.
> For gracious and merciful is he,
>   slow to anger, rich in kindness,
>   and relenting in punishment (Jl 2:13).

• *Gentle, patient servant.* There are four songs of the Suffering Servant or "Servant-of-the Lord" oracles in the book of Isaiah (Is 42:1-41; 49:1-7; 50:4-11; 52:13-53, 12). These sections portray the ideal servant of God whose consecration to the divine will even in the midst of immense sufferings takes away the sins of many. Various interpretations have been offered as to the identification of this Servant. But according to New Testament and Christian tradition, these prophecies are seen as fulfilled, at least most perfectly and completely, in Jesus Christ.[1]

In the first Song of the Suffering Servant, quoted below, we observe this ideal leader, the "chosen one," working to bring about a community of justice or holiness and doing so, among other ways, through prophetic teaching. Nevertheless, he accomplished that mission "modestly and quietly, not whipping people into conformity but transforming them interiorly."[9]

> Here is my servant whom I uphold,
>   my chosen one with whom I am pleased
> Upon whom I have put my spirit;
>   he shall bring forth justice to the nations.
> Not crying out, not shouting,
>   not making his voice heard in the street.

A bruised reed he shall not break,
    and a smouldering wick he shall not quench,
Until he establishes justice on the earth;
    the coastlands will wait for his teachings (Is 42:1-4).

• *The potter and clay.* The image of God as the potter and we as the clay occurs throughout scripture.

In the beginning, "the Lord God formed man out of the clay of the ground" (Gn 2:7). After Jesus' coming, dying and rising, St. Paul mentions that the Savior's followers hold the glorious treasure of the Christian life "in earthen vessels, that the surpassing power may be of God and not from us" (2 Cor 4:7). In those contexts this image communicates the greatness of God and the fragility of humans.

More to the point of our concerns in this book, however, are the uses of the potter and clay notion in the prophets Isaiah and Jeremiah (cf. Is 29:16; 45:9; 64:7; Jr 18:1-10). The latter particularly employs that ancient image to demonstrate God's ability and desire to remake or remold us as soon as we repent of our evil ways. Thus it indicates the importance of conversion if we hope to receive God's blessings and graces.[10] From contemporary experience we know that soft clay can be refashioned over and over again into something new, better and more beautiful; once hardened and baked, however, it becomes fixed. The parallel to the human heart should be obvious. Here is that passage from Jeremiah:

> This word came to Jeremiah from the Lord: Rise up, be off to the potter's house; there I will give you my message. I went down to the potter's house and there he was, working at the wheel. Whenever the object of clay which he was making turned out badly in his hand, he tried again, making of the clay another object of whatever sort he pleased. Then the word of the Lord came to me: Can I not do to you, house of Israel, as this potter has done? says the Lord. Indeed, like clay in the hand of the potter, so are you in my hand, house of Israel. Sometimes I threaten to uproot

and tear down and destroy a nation or a kingdom. But if that nation which I have threatened turns from its evil, I also repent of the evil which I threatened to do. Sometimes, again, I promise to build up and plant a nation or kingdom. But if that nation does what is evil in my eyes, refusing to obey my voice, I repent of the good with which I promised to bless it (Jr 18:1-10).

We can suggest, therefore, that while in the Old Testament there was no room for marginal believers, there were nevertheless frequent teachings about the possibility of repentance. God is even seen as eager to welcome back those who experienced a change of heart. Moreover, the Hebrew scriptures point to the coming Messiah as one who will take a more gentle, modest and quiet approach to those who refuse or are reluctant to accept and follow his message.

New Testament

• *Servant of Yahweh.* At the baptism of Christ in Luke's account, a voice from heaven declared, "You are my beloved Son; with you I am well pleased." Through this allusion to Isaiah 42:1, the evangelist is asserting that Jesus is the Servant of Yahweh, fulfilling the prophecies we cited in the previous section (Lk 3:21-22).[11]

Later, when beginning his public ministry, Jesus entered the synagogue at Nazareth on the Sabbath day, "stood up to read and was handed a scroll of the prophet Isaiah." He unrolled the document and chose for his passage excerpts from Isaiah, chapter 61, starting with "The Spirit of the Lord God is upon me..." (Is 58:6; 61:1-2). After finishing the proclamation, he sat down and said to all those in the synagogue, "Today this scripture passage is fulfilled in your hearing" (Lk 4:16-21). Jesus thus claims that he himself is the Servant of the Lord, fulfilling all those prophecies and thereby inaugurating the messianic era. His mission, however, will be accomplished by pardon, healing and liberation.[12]

• *The gentle, patient Savior.* In the 12th chapter of St. Matthew's gospel, Jesus realized that the Pharisees were scheming to put him to death, and he thereupon withdrew from that place. He cured all who came for help, but warned his recipients not to make him known. The gospel then goes on to state that "this was to fulfill the words spoken through Isaiah the prophet":

> Behold my servant whom I have chosen,
>> my beloved in whom I delight;
> I shall place my spirit upon him,
>> and he will proclaim justice to the Gentiles.
> He will not contend or cry out,
>> nor will anyone hear his voice in the streets.
> A bruised reed he will not break,
>> a smouldering wick he will not quench,
>> until he brings justice to victory.
> And in his name the Gentiles will hope (Mt 12:15-21).

Readers will recognize that quote from Isaiah 42:1-4 which we discussed under our treatment of the Old Testament. However, Matthew's citation does not correspond exactly to the Hebrew, the Septuagint or any one original version. It is the longest Old Testament excerpt in this gospel and is used to suit the author's purpose. Matthew seeks here to emphasize the meekness of Jesus, the Servant of the Lord, and to foretell the extension of Christ's mission to the Gentiles.[13]

The Savior will not contend or wrangle with people, nor speak with vengeful wrath or strident arguments.[14]

He also will not cry out or cry aloud like a dog barks, or a raven croaks, or a drunk bawls or a discontented theater audience roars. Instead of quarrels and shouts, the Servant will be quiet, yet strong, who seeks to conquer by love, not by strife of words.[15]

The Messiah will be gentle with the reed which is bruised and hardly able to stand erect; he will be equally patient with the weak wick whose light is but a flicker. The Christ seeks not to discourage, but to encourage, to heal the wounded reed and nourish it back to health, to nurse along the faint flame until it becomes strong and bright.[16]

• *The wheat and the weeds.* Only Matthew has this particular parable which Jesus taught:

> The kingdom of heaven may be likened to a man who sowed good seed in his field. While everyone was asleep his enemy came and sowed weeds all through the wheat, and then went off. When the crop grew and bore fruit, the weeds appeared as well. The slaves of the householder came to him and said, "Master, did you not sow good seed in your field? Where have the weeds come from?" He answered, "An enemy has done this." His slaves said to him, "Do you want us to go and pull them up?" He replied, "No, if you pull up the weeds you might uproot the wheat along with them. Let them grow together until harvest; then at harvest time I will say to the harvesters, 'First collect the weeds and tie them in bundles for burning; but gather the wheat into my barn'" (Mt 13:24-30).

The weeds sowed by the enemy would have been commonly understood by the people in Palestine at the time of Jesus. Sometimes translated in older versions as "cockle" or "tares," this weed called a bearded darnel was a curse against which farmers in the Holy Land had to labor. In its early stages it so closely resembled wheat that it was impossible to distinguish one from the other. Moreover, as both darnel and wheat grew, their roots became intertwined to such a degree that they could not be separated without tearing up and ruining the good wheat.

As the harvest reached maturity, the darnel, called "bastard wheat" by the Jewish people because of its resemblance to wheat, changed to a slate-grey color. It then could be distinguished from the wheat. Moreover, the two needed to be separated because the bearded darnel was slightly poisonous. It was known to cause dizziness and sickness and it produced a narcotic effect; even in small amounts, it had a bitter and unpleasant taste.

At the end the darnel or weeds were usually separated out by hand, tied into bundles and burned for fuel.[17]

Harvest is a common biblical metaphor for the time of God's judgment. The obvious meaning and commonly accepted interpretation of this parable, therefore, is that Christ was warning his disciples not to anticipate God's final judgment by a definitive exclusion of sinners from the kingdom. Until the Second Coming, the Church will always be a mix of good and evil; it should not, as a consequence, play God by trying to purify itself through purges and harsh judgmental actions. God's own judgment at the end of the ages will eliminate the sinful. Until that moment, the Church's task is to practice patience and preach repentance.[18]

• *Net full of fish.* Shortly after the story of the weeds among the wheat, Matthew offers this very similar parable:

> Again, the kingdom of heaven is like a net thrown into the sea, which collects fish of every kind. When it is full they haul it ashore and sit down to put what is good into buckets. What is bad they throw away. Thus it will be at the end of the age. The angels will go out and separate the wicked from the righteous and throw them into the fiery furnace, where there will be wailing and grinding of teeth (Mt 13:47-50).

There were two main ways of fishing in Palestine — hand casting a net and dragging a net between two boats. In this parable the author envisions the latter approach, which would gather indiscriminately all kinds of fish. Some were clean and some unclean by Levitical standards. Moreover, the mix would be enormous, ranging from 24 to 153 types of fish in the Sea of Galilee alone.

The interpretation parallels that of the weeds and the wheat. The Church until the Second Coming, the end of the ages or the parousia will always include good, fully committed and bad, tenuously connected members. Judgment or separation of the two will come at the final moment, but this remains God's task. Until then, patience and preaching is called for.[19]

• *Lost sheep, misplaced coin and prodigal son.* Luke's Chapter 15 contains these three well-known parables of God's persistent search for the lost or strayed. It begins with the Pharisees and scribes for the third time in Luke complaining that Jesus "welcomes sinners and eats with them" (Lk 15:1). They charged him with encouraging loose morals by associating too freely with those whose lives were not perfect. In their judgment, a believer's duty was to avoid anything or anyone who could soil their sanctity. Christ's response through these parables indicated that God's merciful love does not wait for the sinner's repentance, but actively seeks out his or her restoration.[20]

Sheep tend to stay together, but in the mountainous regions of Palestine one of a flock could little by little nibble its way to an isolated, dangerous location of no return. It was the task of the good shepherd, who knew his sheep, to expend every effort at the end of the day in seeking to find and carry back the lost one to safety.

In the dark, windowless oriental houses a coin could easily be lost among the straw on the floor. A careful housewife would not rest until she found that missing item, even if it meant turning everything upside down.[21]

Pastoral ministers who have struggled with marginal parents and children in religious education programs, including sacramental preparations for first penance, Eucharist and confirmation, will be able easily to identify with the arduous efforts of the conscientious shepherd and careful housewife. So, too, they should find inspiration in the patient, unconditional love of the forgiving father who welcomes back his lost son.

In summary, we could say that the Old and New Testaments urge pastoral leaders to preach clearly the ideals of God's kingdom, but to practice patience with those who fail to live up perfectly to these teachings. They are to act as the Servant of the Lord did. Jesus proclaimed the message with courage, but tempered the proclamation with great love and gentleness, being careful not to break the bruised reed or snuff out the smouldering wick.

The sailor from San Diego experienced that approach and responded positively to it. This navy man could not turn the priest down because he was non-judgmental, patient and compassionate. As a result of the clergyman's gentle Servant of the Lord attitude, the lost son came back to the Church and has not left it.

Guidance from the *Catechism*:

Article 129: "Christians therefore read the Old Testament in the light of Christ crucified and risen.... the New Testament has to be read in the light of the Old.... As an old saying put it, the New Testament lies hidden in the Old and the Old Testament is unveiled in the New" (cf. St. Augustine, *Quaest. in Hept.* 2,73: PL 34, 623; cf. *DV* 16).

Article 978: "...Yet the grace of Baptism delivers no one from all the weakness of nature. On the contrary, we must still combat the movements of concupiscence that never cease leading us into evil" (*Roman Catechism* I, 11, 3).

Article 982: "There is no one, however wicked and guilty, who may not confidently hope for forgiveness, provided his repentance is honest" (*Roman Catechism*, I, 11, 5).

Article 827: "All members of the Church, including her ministers, must acknowledge that they are sinners (Cf. *1 Jn* 1:8-10). In everyone, the weeds of sin will still be mixed with the good wheat of the Gospel until the end of time (Cf. *Mt* 13:24-30). Hence, the Church gathers sinners already caught up in Christ's salvation but still on the way to holiness."

4

The Cruel or Compassionate Church

A friend in my parish has a relative who married a non-Catholic man with no particular Church affiliation. He was willing and wanted to have his wife assume complete responsibility for bringing the children up in the faith. They have raised nine children.

When the eighth child was expected, the wife went to her parish to arrange for the baptism and was told that *both* parents had to attend classes for six weeks before baptism. She explained that her husband was non-Catholic and had given her complete responsibility to raise the children in the faith, but he did not intend to go to meetings. He was holding down two jobs at the time to support his family. The decision remained the same: *both* parents must attend. How lacking in understanding — and lacking in common sense! That child and the ninth baby were not baptized in the Church. (The mother, of course, had baptized them herself.)

She subsequently went to a neighboring parish and explained the circumstances to the pastor. The wife expressed their desire for the sacrament of baptism for the two and was told that "he didn't want to get involved"! The children are now seven and four years old, respectively. Isn't that scandalous? It is to me. It makes me sick at heart. What would Jesus have done?

P.S. I'm a convert, having received instructions, con-
ditional baptism and confirmation at St. John's, Cham-
paign-Urbana in 1944 at the age of 23. Deo Gratias!
— *Illinois*

From his fourth floor office off of East 48th Street in New York City,
Father John Catoir for many years directed the multiple activities
of the Christophers. That position tested his versatile talents and
placed him in constant contact with millions of Americans. Efforts
such as hosting a television show and broadcasting over the radio,
writing a news note for the Christophers publication or handling
enormous correspondence put Catoir in an exceptional position to
catch the prevailing religious attitudes among people in the United
States. That vantage point led him to believe that for many Catholics and non-Catholics in our country, the Church today is not
compassionate and forgiving, but harsh and cruel. Those people see
the Catholic Church "as a stern father, unforgiving and unrelent-
ing in his scolding."[1]

According to Catoir, the Church has performed its necessary
and valid role of trying to be faithful to Jesus' teachings by asserting a right or correct position on issues such as sex, war, peace, capi-
tal punishment and abortion. Nevertheless, in doing so, the Church,
he believes, has failed to communicate the doctrine of God's un-
changing love and mercy. Instead, it conveys the image of a "rigor-
ous institution, tirelessly imposing the full demands of Christian law
upon its members."

To correct that condition and reach out in friendship to the
masses, Father Catoir argues that we must rethink our approach,
"remembering that God loves the sinner but hates the sin. Embracing the sinner is not a sign of laxity. We cannot give moral permission to sinners, but we can try to understand their pain.... The
Church is called to be a comforter of the afflicted and a refuge of
sinners."

A Boston paper's front page coverage of in vitro fertilization
dramatically illustrated this problem of the Church's image. Imme-

diately after the Vatican issued an instruction on respect for human life in its origin, the newspaper carried bold headlines, "Pope Condemns Artificial Procreation."[2] A companion article included photographs of two women with infants in their arms, both children products of the in vitro process. The mothers responded to questions about the Roman document with remarks such as: "This is so typical of the Catholic Church." "How could God not want me to have this beautiful baby!" "God must certainly have blessed what we did to give us such a wonderful child." "That is why I left the Catholic Church long ago."

The Church comes off poorly in such a contrast. It seems uncaring and insensitive to the deep desires of those apparently sterile spouses who wish to have babies, but cannot in the ordinary way. No matter that the Church with this instruction tackled a tough and largely unexplored moral issue. No matter that the *New York Times* editorially approved this attempt of the Church to raise some crucial contemporary questions. No matter that the potentially harmful or at least debatable consequences of artificial procreation, e.g., hired surrogate mothers, future genetic engineering, legal custodial battles, have already begun to surface in this country. No matter. The Church, seeking to be faithful to Christ's words, nevertheless conveyed to many a harsh and cruel impression.

Isolated Events or Frequent Patterns

One need not have recourse to dramatic newspaper stories like this to discover events during which the Church appears unforgiving and inflexible. The letter about baptism from the convert in Illinois is a case in point. Baptismal preparation classes are surely to be encouraged and, as we will state later, even made obligatory for parents. But the rigid insistence on attendance by both mother *and* father described in that note was unfortunate. Regrettable also was the refusal of the neighboring pastor to become involved and the missed opportunity to heal wounds.

While we might dismiss those actions as only the human failure of two specific priests, as isolated tragedies in our very fragile,
fallible Church, further reflection may indicate these are instead
examples of a frequent pastoral pattern in the United States.

Father David O'Rourke, whose journey from Yale to the
priesthood we described earlier, believes that such rigidity and
inflexibility can be traced at least in part to two basically good and
originally praiseworthy factors.[3] One centers around personal commitment and the other involves the faith dimension of a liturgical
celebration.

Personal Commitment and Faith

The personal commitment factor affects both pastoral leaders and individuals seeking the sacraments.

According to O'Rourke's view, many leaders in the Catholic
Church during the past few decades have undergone inner conversions. Through cursillo, marriage encounter or the charismatic
movement, through concern about civil rights, liturgical renewal or
liberation theology, people became deeply, fervently committed to
the Church. That praiseworthy development, however, has had its
down side. Such committed, converted leaders can tend to demand
an equal commitment from every member of the Church and to
display little patience with those whom we would classify as marginal Catholics.

The faith dimension factor springs from the liturgical revisions
of the Second Vatican Council and the subsequent reforms. Wishing to avoid a "magical" use of the sacraments, Church leaders have
established diocesan or parish priorities, policies and programs to
insure that participants receive baptism or marriage with awareness
and faith.

Father O'Rourke himself says, "I have worked to see them
established. I do not find the establishment of policies for baptism
and marriage to be inappropriate. People should understand the
meaning of the motions they are going through."

Nevertheless, when these policies become excessively strict or are rigidly enforced, they can cause spiritual harm and tragic alienation instead of leading people to greater personal conversion and clearer faith awareness. "Good leadership," O'Rourke maintains, "requires that the leader not get too many steps ahead of the people he or she is leading." Insisting on total commitment from participants before ministering baptism or witnessing marriages illustrates that type of "too far ahead" leadership.

As pastor of an inner-city parish in California, the Dominican priest one afternoon suffered through this struggle between the proclaimed ideal and the imperfect reality of sacramental encounters. He had spent the better part of a day in a meeting with the county board of supervisors lobbying against a reduction in the mental health budget. Because of two appointments back at the church, he left the important session early and returned to the rectory.

During the first appointment a couple asked for the baptism of their three variously aged children even though the parents' practice and understanding of the faith were minimal. At the second appointment, a couple living together requested, with some hesitation and confused motives, marriage in the Church.

O'Rourke describes his reactions to the sacramental requests of these marginal Catholics:

> It would have been easy to dismiss each of these couples on the pretext that what they were looking for was something other than baptism or matrimony as we are coming to define them. It was, I admit, especially tempting considering the meeting I left in order to meet with them. And yet, like the poor people who have been turned loose on the city's streets to cope alone, each of these couples was in a spiritual desert looking for something better and dependent on others in order to get it. In their wandering and in their need they are not that different from the generation of people who have been the Church in the past, and whose sometimes thread-thin hanging-on accounts for

our own presence in the Church. The two couples came that afternoon hoping for understanding, knowing they fell short of the ideal, and fearing rejection.

We simply cannot turn people like this away. It would be very arbitrary and cruel. But we are in danger of doing just that. There have been gaps between the leaders and the people of the Church before. This one is more serious because it is being institutionalized on the level of the sacraments which, heretofore, have been one moment at least in which divided peoples have come together.[4]

Overzealous insistence upon firm Church commitment and deep faith awareness, therefore, can partially explain strict parish procedures with regard to the sacraments. However, there is another more subtle, but perhaps more serious reason behind pastoral practices which appear severe and rigid. That reason is the loss of conviction regarding sacramentality in the Church or, in other words, a lack of faith in the power of sacramental actions.

Power of Sacramental Actions

Monsignor Philip Murnion, who guided the Parish Project of the National Conference of Catholic Bishops and now serves as Executive Director of the National Pastoral Life Center in New York City, lists a number of contemporary items which reflect this loss or lack of sacramental conviction or faith.

It seems fair to say that the shift in confirmation to make it a rite in which teenagers give testimony to some kind of commitment has meant the victory of religious educators over liturgists, of word over action. The former have largely been responsible for turning the rite into an expression of commitment already achieved and expressed in various service projects. The rite is not then an occasion for the action of the Spirit so much as an opportunity to testify to compliance with earlier action of the Spirit.

Efforts to make the celebration of the Eucharist an occasion for immediately felt sentiment often suggest that nothing is achieved that is not of our own doing or our own experience.

Strategies regarding baptismal and matrimonial practice often seem motivated not so much by understandings of the sacramentality of these rites as by requirements for the socializing of Church members. How we can use these rites to cultivate more faithful Church practice seems, inadvertently, to take precedence over any understanding that people in practice need the grace of the sacraments.[5]

Underneath these shifts in practical attitudes lies a post Vatican II theological change.

Before the Council, Catholic theology commonly taught that the combined sacramental event of words, objects and actions produced or caused grace. This interaction between God and the human person, as Murnion defines a sacrament, embodies divine and human activity. Therefore, it "has meaning and consequences beyond what we can understand or measure. It also never fully expresses the total reality of this interaction or the communion in the Lord that is the foundations of the action." The action itself, presuming proper dispositions on the part of the recipient and the correct ministering of the ritual, possesses a certain God-given power to convey sanctifying and actual graces as well as a spiritual character in three sacraments.

During the two decades following the Second Vatican Council, some theologians moved away from this causal concept of the sacraments and stressed instead that they were celebrations of a divine action which has already taken place. In the sacrament of penance, for example, the sacramental formula and ritual does not forgive sins, according to this view, but rather celebrates the forgiveness and reconciliation already bestowed by the merciful Christ. Murnion's description of confirmation today is another illustration of that altered sacramental understanding.

This second approach produces several significant practical effects. First, it diminishes the importance of the sacramental rite. Secondly, it places an added burden upon the priest or deacon who celebrates the liturgical event because the value of the ritual depends much more, if not totally, upon the way the sacred ceremonial is carried out. Thirdly, it emphasizes almost exclusively the interior motives and the active participation of recipients. Finally, it weakens the conviction that something more happens during a sacrament than what we can externally perceive or observe on the surface.

From that theological perspective, pastoral leaders find justification in insisting upon policies which require regular participation at Sunday Mass and strong commitment to the Church as conditions for the sacraments. The notion that the sacraments have power within themselves to strengthen or transform the weak and marginal is not necessarily denied, but does not exert a dominant force in parish life.

It should be obvious that we need to strike a balance here. Even if the sacraments do work *ex opere operato* and possess a unique power to confer grace, still the *ex opere operantis* dimension or disposition of the recipient will dictate to a large extent how fruitful or beneficial the sacramental encounter will be. Moreover, God clearly can and does touch the human heart in myriad ways leading up to and following after actual celebration of the sacrament. We need to accept this fact and cultivate those pre- and post-sacramental rites. But having done that, we must step back both in relief and wonder, knowing that Christ's unique presence in the sacraments accomplishes things within human hearts beyond that which we can imagine or perceive.

The fact is, however, that the theological shift in recent decades supplied a supposed theoretical basis for strict and rigid rules about baptism, matrimony and other sacraments. These regulations and their enforcement frequently have caused alienation among people and contributed to the image of the Church as cruel and lacking in compassion.

Church Teaching and Catholic Scholarship

The official teaching of the Church and the ecclesiological reflections of certain contemporary Catholic scholars offer insights on our question about the Church's image: cruel or compassionate.[6] I will examine some of these now.

- *A Consistent and Compassionate Proclamation.*

Pope John Paul II in 1984 succinctly analyzed the tension facing the Church as it seeks to speak faithfully the words of Christ, thereby challenging those who will listen, and at the same time to communicate the mercy of God, which is always available for those who have failed to heed the message but wish to begin again.

The Holy Father notes in this context two equally important principles which coexist and mutually influence one another.

The first principle is that "of compassion and mercy whereby the Church, as the continuer in history of Christ's presence and work... ever seeks to offer, as far as possible, the path of return to God and of reconciliation" with the Creator. The Church does not wish the death of a sinner but that the sinner be converted and live. It is careful "not to bend the bruised reed or to quench the dimly burning wick."[7]

The second principle is "that of truth and consistency, whereby the Church does not agree to call good evil and evil good."[8]

This principle of truth and consistency finds support in the *Dogmatic Constitution on the Church* from the Second Vatican Council. Chapter III, "The Church Is Hierarchical," includes a pivotal section 25 which details the duties of bishops, including the bishop of Rome, as preachers of the gospel, authentic teachers endowed with the authority of Christ and leaders destined to make the faith shine forth, bear fruit and be protected from errors.[9]

The principle of compassion can find support in the documents of Vatican II. The *Decree on the Church's Missionary Activity,* for example, details how the Church must in various ways proclaim the gospel, spread the good news of salvation and make Jesus Christ known who came "to heal the broken-hearted" and "to seek and to save what was lost."[10]

Pope John Paul II underscored the principle of truth and consistency in an exhortation on reconciliation and penance when he stressed the Church's task of preaching. "The Church, since she is the disciple of the one Teacher Jesus Christ, in her own turn, as Mother and Teacher, untiringly exhorts people to reconciliation. And she does not hesitate to condemn the evil of sin, to proclaim the need for conversion...."[11]

He, however, has also stressed the principle of compassion, issuing an encyclical, *Rich in Mercy,* dedicated solely to that topic. In it he says, "The Church of our time... must become more particularly and profoundly conscious of the need to bear witness in her whole mission to God's mercy...."[12]

In *The Reshaping of Catholicism*, theologian and Jesuit Father Avery Dulles upholds the right and need of the Church to follow a principle of truth and consistency.[13] It possesses a specific vision of the world, a unique origin and the means for discharging its mission that are quite different from secular organizations of various kinds. It is centered on Jesus Christ as Lord and Savior and, according to its belief, has been established by the action of God in Jesus Christ. Therefore, Father Dulles writes, "The Church has a deposit of faith that must be maintained intact and transmitted to new members." Moreover, "members of the Church, including the highest officeholders, are not free to change in a substantive way the beliefs, structures, purposes, and forms of worship of the Church. They are trustees, obliged to safeguard the trust committed to them."

But Dulles also espouses that principle of compassion as applied to dissent from official Church teaching. The Church, he says, "can rather easily tolerate internal or privately expressed dissent." In fact, it "as a society that respects the freedom of the human conscience, must avoid procedures that savor of intellectual tyranny." While he maintains that the Church "can scarcely help but oppose public and organized dissent" and will "quite properly seek to minimize the adverse effects of public dissent," he nevertheless has a word of caution for Church leaders.

"Prelates and others who, in their zeal for orthodoxy, would wish to suppress dissent by Draconian measures, might advantageously meditate on the Gospel parable of the good grain and the weeds.... The mistaken doctrines of hierarchical teachers and of theologians can all be considered weeds, but it is not easy, at any given moment, to discern exactly which doctrines are mistaken. For this reason it is often necessary to allow both to survive and to pray that the Holy Spirit will give clarity of insight so that God's truth may in the end prevail."

• *Christ's Sacramental Presence and Power.*

On this issue teachings of the official Church and of certain Catholic scholars have a common theme running through them: The risen Christ is truly present and operative in the sacraments, but the faith, understanding and involvement of the participants will largely determine any sacrament's effectiveness.

The *Constitution on the Sacred Liturgy* teaches that the sacraments "do, indeed, confer grace." It goes on in the same sentence, however, to mention that "the very act of celebrating them most effectively disposes the faithful to receive this grace to their profit, to worship God duly, and to practice charity."

As a consequence of this doctrine, therefore, the bishops urge that it is of "the greatest importance that the faithful should easily understand the sacramental signs...."[14]

Article 7 of that same document provides, according to one consultant at the Second Vatican Council, the doctrinal basis for all of the liturgical reforms which were to follow. This paragraph proclaims that "Christ is always present in his Church, especially in her liturgical celebrations.... By his power he is present in the sacraments so that when anybody baptizes it is really Christ himself who baptizes." In a subsequent article, the Constitution maintains that "from the liturgy, therefore, and especially from the Eucharist, grace is poured forth upon us as from a fountain..." (art. 10).

Nevertheless, the Vatican II text cautions that if the liturgy is "to produce its full effects it is necessary that the faithful come to it with proper dispositions, that their minds be attuned to their voices, and that they cooperate with heavenly grace lest they receive it in vain" (art. 11).

As we would expect, the actual renewed rites mirror in specific ways those generic principles.

The Christian Initiation ritual, for instance, states that baptism incorporates us into Christ, raises us from a natural human condition to the dignity of adopted children, forgives all our sins, makes us a new creation, links together all who have been signed by it, makes us sharers in God's own life and marks us with an indelible, unchangeable effect.

However, through careful instruction and preparation for the baptism, "in the actual celebration, the people of God (represented not only by the parents, godparents and relatives, but also, as far as possible, by friends, neighbors, and some members of the local church) should take an active part."[15]

Pope John Paul II, echoing the introductory words of the *Rite of Marriage*, speaks of the sacramental effects of matrimony. It "takes up again and makes specific the sanctifying grace of baptism." "It is not exhausted in the actual celebration of the sacrament of marriage, but rather accompanies the married couple throughout their lives." By it Christian spouses "are fortified and receive a kind of consecration." It confers on them "the grace and moral obligation" to transform their whole lives.[16]

Still, he also advises that "the liturgical celebration of marriage should involve the whole community, with the full, active and responsible participation of all those present...."[17]

Avery Dulles summarizes in his *Models of the Church* what has been a traditional view of the sacraments. They are signs of grace, signs pointing to something invisible, but "full" signs, signs of something really present. Moreover, they are efficacious signs, signs (or symbols) which produce or intensify that of which they are signs. The sacraments contain the grace they signify, and confer the grace they contain.[18]

Liturgist Mark Searle, seeking to construct an empirically based theory of what the liturgy is and does, hints at both the power of the sacramental rite and the need for our openness to it. "The rite is something to be done; what matters primarily is that it be done.... The meaning is in the ritual itself; authenticity merely requires allowing your mind, heart, and behavior to be shaped by the rite.... It is not what I bring to the rite that matters so much as what happens to me during and what I come away from it with.... The faith celebrated in the liturgy is the faith of the Church, which in turn is none other than the faith of Christ."[19]

• *A Community of Different Disciples.*

In 1943 Pope Pius XII issued his encyclical on the Mystical Body of Christ and in effect started a trend of theological thought which, over the next decade, would view the Church as an organic, communal mystery, and not solely a structured institution. The bishops at the Second Vatican Council continued that emphasis. The *Dogmatic Constitution on the Church* in its first chapter treats "The Mystery of the Church" and in the following chapter pursues the biblically inspired concept of the Church as the People of God.[20] At the Extraordinary Synod of 1985, the participants' final report warned about describing or treating the Church "as a purely institutional structure devoid of her mystery."[21]

The Church as mystery cannot, therefore, be captured by any one image, model, category or theory; no one concept exhausts its meaning or can do it full justice. They all complement one another and compensate for one another's shortcomings.[22] If one concept is exaggerated, it results in a distorted understanding of the Church; but when we combine them all together, we get a richer, fuller grasp of what the Church is.

Having established those cautions, we want to observe that

Pope John Paul II through a passing remark in his first encyclical suggested a then new idea of the Church as a "community of disciples." He also, however, indicated that each member of this community is different, every person following Christ as a disciple "at times very consciously and consistently, at other times not very consciously and not very consistently."[23]

We find the pertinent phrase in the Acts of the Apostles: "So the Twelve called together the community of the disciples..." (Ac 6:2). While the notion of a "community of disciples" does not occur in the documents of Vatican II, those texts do call Church members "disciples" more than 20 times. The concept has grown in popularity with the bishops of the United States who, for example, employed "community of disciples" in both their 1983 and 1986 pastorals, *The Challenge of Peace* and *Economic Justice for All.* Moreover, Avery Dulles has given the idea rather extensive treatment in two publications.[24]

In his analysis, Dulles notes how during Jesus' life there were degrees of intimacy among the disciples of Christ. Some were clearly closer to the Master than others; some have more specific tasks assigned to them. In addition, their response to Christ's call, their understanding of his message and their fidelity to his demands were uneven and flawed. Even Jesus could not secure a 100 percent success rate in his preaching ministry.

Dulles observes how in the post-Easter community of disciples during the early centuries, the Church proposed and often received a demanding and heroic way of life from its members. After the conversion of Constantine, this heroism disappeared as a common trait of Christians. While the ideal of discipleship never vanished, there was greater accommodation to the ordinary patterns of society at that time.

According to Dulles' concept, a member of the Church is a disciple of Jesus, a person following Christ, an individual entering into a relationship with the Lord. But by the very fact that it is a relationship, the connection with Jesus is a fragile one, founded entirely on faith; it is also a precarious one, because it is always possible for a disciple to betray or deny the Master; moreover, it is not a static condition, but a continual movement requiring each day a fresh grace from God, ongoing conversions and repeated efforts to go forward; it is, therefore, never a fully successful, completely perfect journey. The Church, in this model, stands as deficient, always in need of correction.

The sacrament of penance, when examined from this model, "is the ceremony at which those who have fallen short of the demands of discipleship, and have repented, are reintegrated into the community, somewhat as Peter, the prototypical disciple, was mercifully restored to his position of leadership after having betrayed Jesus."[25]

Scripture scholar Raymond E. Brown has studied the Church in the last part of the first century as described in Matthew's gospel. He discovers there also the Church as a community of different or "mixed" disciples.[26]

According to Brown, Matthew is the only gospel that uses the word "church." But that church or assembly is, in the evangelist's view, able to or at least should mix and blend quite contrasting groups of people: Jewish and Gentile Christians, rich and poor people, saints and sinners.

It is Matthew also who uses the parable of the weeds growing among the wheat, which we analyzed at length in the preceding chapter. The Matthean Jesus warns that a purge as suggested in the parable might "damage the good members, and so the situation must be tolerated until there comes a divine judgment. Sects can pride themselves on a purism that drives out all who do not meet an ideal, but a church has to show patience and mercy."[27]

In the parable describing a search for the one stray sheep, Matthew's text gives instructions about the pastoral obligation toward a misled member of the community. Unlike the standard values of organized society, the pastoral leader symbolized by the shepherd must reflect the values of Jesus who came to save lost sinners.[28]

Matthew finally gives a strong teaching about forgiving the

brother who sins against us (Mt 18:21-22). The seventy times seven figure means an infinite number and this Matthean parable consequently harshly rebukes those in the Church who refuse forgiveness.

The Church is indeed a community of different disciples, of saints and sinners, of committed and uncommitted, of hot, lukewarm and cold followers of Christ.

Elitist or Messy Church

Both Raymond Brown and Avery Dulles would concur with John Catoir's question about the cruel or compassionate Church which opened this chapter.

Brown maintains that "lest it be accused of laxness, the Church is often very careful about forgiving. Yet, the number of people who have turned away from the Church because they found it too forgiving is infinitesimal; the members who have turned away because they found it unforgiving is legion."[29]

Dulles comments, "To large numbers of young people, and to others not so young, the laws and dogmas of the Church seem designed to control and crush rather than to nourish and satisfy the needs of the spirit."[30]

When the Parish Project mentioned earlier ended, the last issue of its newsletter *Parish Ministry* included summary remarks by Monsignor Philip Murnion. In those comments he spoke about a "messy" or an "elitist" Catholic Church.[31]

Traditionally, the Church has viewed itself and operated as a "messy" faith family made up of all types within the same parish. There are, Murnion insists, half-hearted and whole-hearted members; there are sinners and others trying to be holy; there are lukewarm Catholics and hot Catholics. The Church has been able to include these disparate elements and yet at the same time, within that inclusiveness, to keep posing the ideal and examples and models of virtue that all its members strive for in their lives.

Murnion judges that there is a slight tendency in our times

to move away from that style into an exclusive, elitist approach. Today, nearly two decades after his essay, I would judge that movement more than a slight tendency, but still not at present a major thrust. Regardless of how strong or slight this tendency may be, it still suggests that "the only real members of the Church are those who make some kind of full commitment as adults." Moreover, the sacraments are considered "for those already deeply involved in the life of faith, not for the ones who are struggling."

Murnion cautions against this "elitist" style and urges the retention of our "messy" approach, one which holds that the Church was created primarily for sinners, that it can be "as open as possible to who we are" and at the same time "as encouraging as possible to what we can become."

Is the Catholic Church cruel or compassionate, elitist or messy, stern or gentle, unbending or forgiving, rigid or flexible? These are different words and different questions, but a certain similarity exists among those inquiries and several common issues thread through them all. We will now see how Church laws strike a balance between truth and consistency, compassion and mercy.

Guidance from the *Catechism*

Article 1122: "…The preaching of the Word is required for the sacramental ministry itself, since the sacraments are sacraments of faith, drawing their origin and nourishment from the Word" (*PO* 4 §§ 1, 2)

Article 1123: "Because they are signs they also instruct. They not only presuppose faith, but by words and objects they also nourish, strengthen, and express it. That is why they are called 'sacraments *of faith*'" (*SC* 59).

Article 1127: "Celebrated worthily in faith, the sacraments confer the grace that they signify (cf. Council of Trent (1547): DS 1605; DS 1606). They are *efficacious* because in them Christ himself is at work: it is he who baptizes, he who acts in his sacraments in order to communicate the grace that each sacrament signifies."

Article 1128: "From the moment that a sacrament is celebrated in accordance with the intention of the Church, the power of Christ and his Spirit acts in and through it, independently of the personal holiness of the minister. Nevertheless, the fruits of the sacraments also depend on the disposition of the one who receives them."

5   Laws and Life

*W*hen I prepared for my son's baptism, I chose my cousin as godmother. She had helped me greatly in my pregnancy. She gave me a book early on that prepared me for later stages and birth. She rounded up maternity clothes from friends and baby clothes her children and others had worn. She gave me a surprise shower of baby gifts and made sure to invite all my family and friends to share the joy and provide the rest of my then baby-to-be's needs. She put me on her sofa and fed me a liquid diet when I came down with a winter virus for which I could take no medicine. All this while she and her husband provided for their own five children.

I hoped that when I asked her to be my son's godmother I would be able to honor her and partially express my gratitude. But I also chose her because she was Catholic and because she saw to it that her own five children attended Catholic schools (at great financial hardship), that they attended church and received the sacraments even though she and her husband had never married in the Church and rarely went to Mass.

She was honored. She bought Danny (my son) a beautiful suit to wear for his baptism. She offered us her home and help for a party afterward. Then she phoned me in tears to tell me her pastor had refused to let her be godmother unless she promised to marry in the Church. She had seen the marriages of friends break up after they were "blessed" by the Church and had a superstitious fear that it would happen to hers. I thought the fear irrational and silly. I figured the divorces following sacramental marriages were either coincidental or that the "blessing" of those marriages were last ditch attempts to shore up those already in trouble. But I didn't think she was silly because her fear was real to her.

I told her I'd go with her to see the pastor to try to change his mind. I had formerly belonged to the same parish and knew the old monsignor in question to be very strict but also a caring man of God. She said she would take instructions in preparation for the sacramental marriage but wouldn't promise to then follow through, and she didn't think her husband would participate.

Well, I argued that she practiced Christian charity to me and to anyone in need, that if I were unable to she would see to my child's Catholic upbringing and that her own children's upbringing showed some practice of the faith.

He refused totally to allow her to be a godmother without a paper from him. He said she "lived in sin" and until she decided to change that, he'd have nothing to do with her. Her offer to compromise was unacceptable.

She left in tears again and in shame. I left angry. I felt as mother of the baptized child I had some choice and that, even though a lay person, I was a member of the Church and so was my cousin (though her participation was through a weekly envelope and her children). I didn't think the Church was, or even should be, a democracy but neither was it or should it be an autocracy.

So I went to my parish priest. He said he wouldn't personally go against another priest. But, if I could find a priest who would allow my cousin as godmother the baptism could take place there and be recorded there. Through a friend who is a nun I found a priest who listened to the story and agreed my cousin would be a good godparent. He baptized my son. I hoped the words of the ceremony would witness to my cousin. I hope they did. I know her pastor's words did, since I heard her tell more than one person that she was "not allowed in church" because of her marriage.   — *Pennsylvania*

The very strict old monsignor mentioned in the above letter, who was "also a caring man of God," would probably cite Church legislation in defense of his refusal to allow this woman "living in sin" to act as a godmother for baptism.

Canon 874 of the current *Code of Canon Law* states that a sponsor must "be a Catholic who has been confirmed and has already received the sacrament of the Most Holy Eucharist and leads a life in harmony with the faith and the role to be undertaken."

The pastor who said he "wouldn't personally go against another priest" might have pointed to another code, number 519, which gives him responsibility and authority only over the community entrusted to him as shepherd of that parish. He could thus argue that the cousin in question, married out of the Church and residing in another parish, is not under his care.

Why did the priest, recommended by a nun, approve of the cousin as a godparent and baptize the baby? Was he the kind of cleric who wants to be popular and automatically, indiscriminately goes along with people's wishes? Or did he find in Church law rules which would justify his course of action?

In this chapter we will explore the ever-present tension between all laws and daily life, a tension exemplified by our case of the woman's desire for her cousin who "married out of the Church" to serve as a baptismal sponsor. We will discover that while Church or canon law contains clear and definite rules for the behavior of Catholic Christians, it provides, at the same time, a surprising flexibleness and compassionate applicability.

How, then, may and should rules of Church law, like canons 874, 519 and other related legislation, be interpreted and applied in practice?

Church or Canon Law

One could say that the goals or purposes of Church law are as follows: to facilitate the process by which an individual moves through grace to the ultimate glory of salvation; to foster the building of a Catholic Christian community bound together by ties of faith and love; and to help bring about Jesus' desired kingdom of truth, justice and peace.[1] In spite of evident differences between contemporary secular law and our sacred legal system, differences which we will examine below, their goals and purposes manifest certain real similarities. Both seek to enshrine, protect and foster good constructive values.

Positive and Negative Emphasis

Having said this, however, we can maintain that, whereas Church law overall displays a fundamentally positive thrust, secular legal systems have, at least in the minds of most people, a basically negative orientation.[2] Church laws generally promote virtuous deeds which contribute to the fulfillment of their goals. Secular legislation, on the other hand, generally prohibits violent acts which undercut or frustrate the realization of its purposes.

As an illustration of this emphasis, universal Church legislation about marriage states that "pastors of souls are obliged to see to it that their own ecclesial community furnishes the Christian faithful assistance so that the matrimonial state is maintained in a Christian spirit and makes progress toward perfection."[3] It then suggests four specific ways for providing this aid.

As an illustration of the contrary trend of secular laws, the following story from a daily newspaper dramatizes their often negative nature.

> When it comes to building a lawful, orderly society, every little bit helps.

Michael Bragman did his part Friday, when Governor Mario Cuomo signed into law the assemblyman's bill to help prevent the theft of shopping carts.

The law imposes a $100 fine for every shopping cart, milk crate or other container you've ever stolen from a supermarket.

Bragman said the cost of replacing stolen carts and crates reaches into the millions of dollars each year, and those costs translate into higher grocery bills for consumers.

There's no need for repentant shopping cart thieves to despair, however. The law includes an 80-day "amnesty" period during which carts and containers can be returned with no questions asked.

And you can still wheel your groceries home in a store cart if you get written permission from the store and promise to return it promptly.

Besides shopping carts and milk cartons, the law covers bakery trays, egg baskets, laundry carts and poultry baskets.[4]

These, of course, are generalizations, with the opposite tone of the law a reality on occasion.

Thus, some secular laws do bear a positive and promotional thrust. For example, certain laws are designed to establish institutions such as banks, corporations and administrative agencies. Other laws empower, such as contract law or the law allowing a person to make a will. These laws allow private persons to make rules for themselves and their affairs.

Moreover, some Church rules do carry a negative and prohibiting tenor. For example, canon 860 states that baptism is not to be conferred in private houses or hospitals unless there is some necessity and the local bishop approves. Another canon, number 1072, directs pastors of souls to dissuade young people from entering marriage before the age customary in the region.

Nevertheless, most people tend to consider sacred laws for the greater part as positive and promoting. They likewise think that secular legal systems are negative and prohibiting, with criminal law as typical.

We can see the constructive tone of Church laws as logically developing from God's revelation to us through the Bible.

Both Jesus and St. Paul acknowledged and endorsed the legal directives of the Old Testament.[5] "Do not think that I have come to abolish the law or the prophets. I have come not to abolish but to fulfill" (Mt 5:17). "Are we then annulling the law by this faith? Of course not! On the contrary, we are supporting the law" (Rm 3:31). Moreover, Paul clearly stressed the importance of discipline within the Church of God, as we see in his first letter to the Corinthians (1 Cor 5-6).

But both Christ and the Apostle to the Gentiles emphasize positive commandments or laws.

> "Teacher, which commandment in the law is the greatest?"
> He said to them, "You shall love the Lord, your God, with all your heart, with all your soul, and with all your mind. This is the greatest and the first commandment. The second is like it: You shall love your neighbor as yourself. The whole law and the prophets depend on these two commandments" (Mt 22:34-40).

Paul echoes those words of his Master: "Owe nothing to anyone, except to love one another; for the one who loves another has fulfilled the law.... Love does no evil to the neighbor; hence, love is the fulfillment of the law" (Rm 13:8-10).

Church laws naturally reflect this positive and love emphasis of Christ and St. Paul, an orientation which differs from the generally perceived negative thrust of secular legislation. But the Church's legal system varies even more radically from the secular body of laws which surround us in the United States, Canada and other English-speaking countries.

More General Comparisons

The secular law system we live under tends to be extremely complicated, even confusing and yet quite versatile. It is fluid, constantly shifting and efficiently flexible. General principles are revered, but limited in number. Statutes abound and are amended frequently. Legislation is often detailed, even ornate, anticipating as many contingencies as possible. The result is an extremely active legal system, consisting of a complex though manageable succession of laws and jurisprudence.[6]

Canon or Church law, on the other hand, tends to be clear and simple. It emphasizes written principles which are less complex, but not as flexible as secular laws. They are not easily or often changed. Instead, they need interpretation and application to achieve their purposes.[7]

We can see these fundamental differences reflected in the published bodies of existing laws within both systems. The number of volumes containing current secular laws, cases and interpretations in a lawyer's office or law professor's study will overwhelm the uninitiated visitor. On the contrary, the Church's basic body of legislation, the 1917 *Code of Canon Law* and now the 1983 *Code of Canon Law*, is published in a single relatively small bound book. The most recent edition, for example, contains less than 2,000 canons which touch nearly every structure of the Roman Catholic Church. Moreover, many of these are not statutes or laws strictly speaking, but more exhortative or theological statements.[8]

Interpretation and Application

A further difference between the secular and sacred systems, and one critical to the issues under consideration in this book, revolves around the matter of interpretation and application. The *Code of Canon Law* generally remains on the level of principles rather than offering detailed regulations.[9] One canon lawyer summarizes the consequences of this tendency and compares it with the secular legal approach in these words:

> To achieve Church order, the Code frequently relies on the exercise of discretion by ecclesiastical administrators in applying the law to concrete situations. The administrator is called upon to humanize and accommodate the legislator's canonical principles, set them in their proper context, apply them equitably, and dispense from them whenever pastorally necessary. Civil law also expresses general principles to which administrators must be sensitive, but their discretionary application of such principles is more often circumscribed by an everexpanding complexus of statutory legislation, administrative procedure, and case law.[10]

All these differences between the sacred and the secular legal systems cause complications with the everyday life of the Catholic Church in English-speaking countries, especially the United States. Our attitude toward secular law understandably influences and molds our attitude toward Church law, despite their radical differences. We often, as a result, fail to understand the multiple kinds of Church laws currently in force and the many ways the Church provides for applications, interpretations and exemptions.

We now examine these major types of Church laws with their variable binding obligations. Then we will explore the many types of exceptions provided in the canonical system.

Types of Church Laws

The discussion in this book centers on liturgical celebrations — more precisely, baptism and marriage, but also, by extension, first penance and first Eucharist, confirmation and Christian burial. Church laws which regulate the general liturgy and these particular rites appear in the 1983 *Code of Canon Law*, in the Introduction and rubrics of each ritual book, and in specific decrees issued by the appropriate universal, national or diocesan Church authorities.

Contemporary scholars divide these numerous regulations into two categories: "theological statements" and "juridic norms."[11]

Theological statements are not truly legal in nature although they appear in texts of Church law. They include divine law statements from an ecumenical council, the Bible or natural law, statements of authentic Church teaching that are not divinely revealed dogma, and statements that are mere theological opinions subject to dispute and debate among scholars.[12]

These usually occur at the beginning of a major section in the *Code of Canon Law* and the introduction or Praenotanda of each liturgical book.

The *Code of Canon Law*, for example, starts its treatment of baptism with this theological statement:

> Baptism, the gate to the sacraments, necessary for salvation in fact or at least in intention, by which men and women are freed from their sins, are reborn as children of God and, configured to Christ by an indelible character, are incorporated in the Church, is validly conferred only by washing with true water together with the required form of words.[13]

Juridic norms are properly legal in character although they can have varying degrees of importance and binding force. These deal with norms of action, regulations governing Church structures, legal principles, procedural rules, rights and obligations, penal laws, etc.[14]

They can be placed in the following categories:

• *Preceptive* norms impose a binding obligation on subjects of the law, even though they contain varying degrees of obligatory force.[15]

• *Exhortations* are preceptive norms which use the subjunctive. They normally speak of an ideal way of acting in general, rather than of a single action or other specific matter. These uphold a value, without specifying exactly how it is to be attained.[16]

• *Recommendations* do not impose any obligation. They express an ideal or preferred manner of acting, but leave it to the subject of the law to decide whether to observe this ideal. There are relatively few of them, because law by nature intends to impose binding obligations.[17]

• *Discretionary* or *facultative* norms, common in our current liturgical law, permit options, but alternatives from which one must choose. The marriage ritual, to illustrate, contains a rich variety of prayers, formulas and blessings; however, the bride and groom are expected to select one from each of the options offered and not search for different texts from some other source.[18]

• *Statements of rights* allow a certain action to be taken or not to be taken as the person affected desires. These differ from discretionary norms because, while alternatives or options are offered, there is no obligation to accept any of them.[19]

• *Statements of capabilities* specify who is capable of holding a certain office or performing a certain function. This, however, does not mean everyone so qualified has a right to that office or function. They must first be designated by a competent authority as qualified and needed for such service in the Church.[20]

This overview description of Church laws should clearly reveal their great variety both in kind and in the obligations they impose or the binding force they possess. Consequently, it is critical, first of all, that pastoral leaders gain a thorough understanding of those norms which pertain to their work. Sometimes the clergy and others in leadership roles have imposed needless restrictions on people and caused unnecessary hardships simply through lack of knowledge about existing legal directives. They were unaware of the many options and nuances contained in Church law.

For example, to return to our case of the cousin godmother in Pennsylvania, there are three canons which deal with baptismal sponsors, one of which has seven subdivisions. The first begins with this qualifying phrase, "Insofar as possible...."[21] The second canon declares that one sponsor is sufficient, with two the maximum number allowed (canon 873). A third canon states that "a baptized person who belongs to a non-Catholic ecclesial community may not be admitted except as a witness to baptism and together with a Catholic sponsor" (canon 874, no. 2). Those alone open up possibilities for solutions to complex or difficult situations like the one described in our introductory letter.

Exceptions, Adaptations and Exemptions

In addition, however, the Church has always, under the 1917 *Code of Canon Law* and in the modernized 1983 version as well, offered legal exceptions, adaptations or exemptions to existing norms. While upholding the law, thus maintaining the principle of consistency and truth, the Church still recognizes the uniqueness of each human situation and legalizes various ways of relief from the law in those circumstances, thus manifesting the principle of compassion and mercy.[22] These ways of relief include:

• *Matters of minimal significance.* There is a Latin canonical axiom which traces its origin back to Roman law: *De minimis non curat praetor.* Laws or norms as well as judges or officials should not be concerned about negligible matters or issues of minimal significance. That might be translated into the earthy adage: "Don't sweat the small stuff."

• *Nature of the document and directives.* As we have seen, current Church liturgical law appears in a variety of forms, some binding, some not. Moreover, such norms originate from sources of differing importance. A regulation in the ritual book, to illustrate, carries more weight than a private response from a Vatican office to a local bishop on a specific matter.

• *Custom and usage.* Both the 1917 and 1983 *Codes of Canon Law* state that local custom or usage is the best interpreter of laws.[23] While the canons limit the development of legal customs, factual custom — the actual usage of the Spirit-guided community — helps underscore the fact that such a way of acting can be the clearest sign of what may be needed for Church order and discipline.

• *Cessation of law.* While this may occur through contrary legal customs or the introduction of new law, canonists agree also that when a Church law, canon or decree has become obsolete or useless, it is no longer a law. Although an arbitrary invoking of this principle can be perilous for order in the Church, its existence does underscore the need for community acceptance of Church law.

• *Dispensation from the law.* The Second Vatican Council introduced a movement toward subsidiarity or decentralization in the Church. A practical effect of this was to extend the power of the local bishop to dispense the faithful for their spiritual good and in particular cases from the general law of the Church.

This relaxation of a merely ecclesiastical law in a particular case, done for the spiritual good of the faithful, extends to all disciplinary laws except the few reserved to the Apostolic See. For validity the dispensation requires a just and reasonable cause.[24]

• *Epieikeia.* This hard to translate Greek word occurs in Paul's letter to the Philippians. He says to them, "Your kindness should be known to all" (Ph 4:5). Instead of kindness, other translations term it considerateness, forebearance, fairness, gracious gentleness, softness.[25]

The Greeks said that *epieikeia* should enter when strict justice becomes unjust because of its generality. "There may be individual instances when a perfectly just law becomes unjust or where justice is not the same thing as equity." A person has the quality of *epieikeia* if that individual knows when not to apply the strict letter of the law, when to relax justice and introduce mercy.[26]

Aristotle introduced this idea in the context of his reflections on justice in the *Nicomachean Ethics.* The very nature of every law means that in some cases it may grant imperfect justice or no justice at all. All law is universal; but about some things it is not possible to make a universal statement which shall be correct. The scope of *epieikeia* "is to bring a corrective into the application of law whenever it is so warranted."[27]

In the Church, *epieikeia* is not exercised by Church authority, but by those who are trying to observe the prescriptions of Church discipline. It has been defined as a "correction or emendation of a law which in its expression is deficient by reason of its universality, a correction made by a subject who deviates from the clear words of the law." To make such judgments and act upon them may be an act of virtue, discerning the deeper purpose of Church discipline.[28]

• *Excusing causes.* Long before the Second Vatican Council, canon lawyers and moral theologians recognized and taught how one might be "excused" from observance of Church law. Serious inconvenience or damage in proportion to the law could make it a moral impossibility for a person to keep the law in question and, thus, that individual would be excused from it.

Interpretation

We finally come to the question of interpreting these far-ranging and diverse Church laws, laws which admit of so many exceptions and adaptations.

Here is precisely where the tension between the Anglo-American legal mindset and the European-Roman Church law attitude becomes acute.

A Church lawyer and expert in canon law, maintains that Americans, including American Catholics, have this view of law:

> Although they realize that law is very complicated, they believe that it should make sense. If it does not make sense, it should be changed as soon as possible. Most Americans consider law to be supreme. No one should be above the law. There should be few exceptions; all citizens should be treated equally by the law. Laws should be written in such a way that their application is predictable. Thus, they should be marked by reasonableness and should cover many details. This view of law can sometimes cause people

to interpret individual laws too literally. If the law addresses many contingencies, what need is there for "interpretations" of its meaning or special exceptions? Administrators should not easily or often grant exemptions from the law. If this occurs, the law is defective. Legislators can solve some such problems, administrators others, but the final word belongs to the judge. When all other remedies fail, the individual who deserves an exemption goes to court.[29]

The following incident in Modesto, California, typifies that tendency to interpret individual laws too literally:

> People heading for work were confronted by a train that remained stalled across a street for almost two hours during rush hour Monday because its crew had reached the maximum hours it could work legally.
> A Union Pacific spokesman confirmed that a Tidewater Southern freight was stalled because of a communications mixup over crews. One crew had worked the maximum 12 hours allowed under federal law, and another crew wasn't called soon enough to get to Modesto in time, said Ron Ahearn, manager of Union Pacific's terminal operations in Stockton.[30]

Would not the short amount of time needed to move the train away from intersections in the middle of town have been an acceptable deviation from the law and more in keeping with the mind of the original lawgiver?

American Catholics carry a similarly strict attitude toward Church law. All those exceptions and exemptions in canonical legislation described above, for instance, run contrary to the legal milieu in which we live.

This rigid approach, however, differs from the longstanding axiom in canon law which states that "favors are to be multiplied; burdens are to be restricted." The official Catholic legal system encourages people to interpret the law broadly when this is favorable to them, but requires a strict interpretation when individual rights or other values may be compromised or harmed.[31]

Moreover, we have a new development which suggests a more open and wider style of obedience to Church legislation, especially liturgical laws. The *Constitution on the Liturgy* states on the one hand that "no other person, not even a priest, may add, remove, or change anything in the liturgy on his own authority."[32] But it earlier declared that, "pastors of souls must, therefore, realize that, when the liturgy is celebrated, something more is required than the laws governing valid and lawful celebration. It is their duty also to ensure that the faithful take part fully aware of what they are doing, actively engaged in the rite and enriched by it" (art. 11).

Some liturgical scholars consider that this obligation imposed by the Church upon pastors to bring about "something more" implies a "new type of obedience." Pastoral leaders today, with flexible liturgical books and principles, must be "liturgically creative and responsive to pastoral needs without being antinomian and frivolously iconoclastic." They should "maintain fidelity to clearly established norms while being pastorally responsible." They may need to go beyond the precise, specific norm for the sake of the larger, ultimate goal of bringing the liturgy to life for the people.[33]

Catholic Discomfort

We have noted here and there in our analysis of Church or canon law how American Catholics experience discomfort and difficulty interpreting and applying canonical rules. This phenomenon occurs despite the often built-in flexibility of those regulations and the Church's official encouragement of open-ended interpretations. Why is that so? We offer the following reasons:

   a. Church or canon law is more closely related to European civil law than to Anglo-American common law. Both Church and European law have roots in Roman law.

b. Since our secular legislation has always been construed in the common law tradition as opposed to the European tradition, we tend to approach the Church's written law as legislation designed to be strictly construed as it is in the common law tradition.

c. The law the average American has greatest familiarity with is criminal law, which has a fundamentally negative purpose of prohibiting undesirable conduct. As a consequence, we tend to approach law, including Church law, as a set of prohibitions to be strictly applied.

We will examine these three points more closely in the material which follows.

Secular Legal Systems

There are two contemporary secular legal systems with which we are most familiar: European, Roman or civil law and Anglo-American, English or common law.

Both share the view that a system of laws accepted, understood and obeyed by members of a particular society or community is good and, more, necessary for society's survival. They protect the rights of individuals; they enable citizens or members to live in peace and harmony, and they promote the common good and the goals which that society, community or organization seeks to obtain.

But both also recognize these qualifying and sobering truths:

- Secular laws are the products of limited and flawed human minds. Consequently, no legal decree is perfect.
- Laws tend to lag behind life; legislation cannot keep pace with society's ceaseless behavioral shifts or people's constantly changing customs.
- Laws never are able adequately to cover every individual case or circumstance.

Both legal systems, therefore, attempt to achieve the purposes of good laws while simultaneously making provisions for these limitations of every legislative enactment. They do so, however, in quite different ways.

European or Roman Law

The European, Roman or civil law system is based on the legal traditions, concepts and vocabularies of ancient Rome. At one time, mainly for commercial reasons, there was a search to discover some arrangement of rules applicable to all the persons of diverse origins living in the Roman empire. Leaders sought to determine what principles might be common to every legal system. If these could be established, then, in their view, a perfect, universal set of laws would be possible.[34]

This led to an approach which drafted legislation and built up a comprehensive system of laws that centered around major principles rather than detailed rules. It enshrined generic values instead of proposing specific regulations. These tendencies resulted in comprehensive codifications legislatively imposed from which courts derived all the rules by which cases were decided. According to this system, judicial decisions were not of themselves an original source of legal rules.[35]

In the European or Roman judicial approach, the judge studies the sweeping, universal and timeless law, then applies, adapts and interprets it to particular circumstances. This is a crucial point in our discussion here. The role of the judge in applying and interpreting European written law to the complexities of an individual situation parallels the role of the bishop, priest or Church official in applying and interpreting Church law pastorally to the complexities of the Christian life with its various stages or phases of conversion. We will draw out that comparison in a moment.

English or Anglo-American Law

American law is inherited from the English. To distinguish from European, civil law, it is known as common law. The common law in England was the judge-made law which developed in the central or royal courts and was common to all of England. Characteristically, English and American law is made by judges deciding disputes on a case-by-case basis. The decision in a previous case becomes a precedent or authority which judges normally follow in subsequent cases. While judges in European civil law courts arrive at sometimes unique solutions to the disputes before them, their decisions do not create new law. Rather, they purport to be interpreting and applying the general principles and rules of the civil code. Common law judges, in contrast, often make decisions without legislation and these decisions themselves establish principles and rules to be applied in future cases.[36]

During the 800 years in which the common law was developed by English and American judges, there was little legislation. When Parliament did enact new law, the judges resented it and perceived it as an intrusion on their work. For this reason, the judges tended to interpret legislation narrowly and inflexibly. For example, a famous maxim for statutory interpretation states that statutes (that is legislation) in derogation of or altering the common law should be strictly construed. Because legislation was resented by common law judges, they tended to look to the letter of written statutory law rather than the spirit.

We have inherited in our culture that narrow approach to written or statutory law and we often misunderstand Church law because we treat it as common law judges for 800 years treated legislation. We should understand that the Church's canon law more closely resembles European, civil law. Most law of the European civil system is written in the form of general principles and rules which judges are meant to interpret and apply flexibly to the many different and complex problems presented to them in their courts.

Flexibility, as well as consistency, is important in any legal system. The Anglo-American, common law systems achieve flexibility by giving judges the power to develop new rules or precedents as new and different problems are presented in the courts. The judges also have the power to abandon old precedents or rules established in earlier cases. Consistency is achieved in the common law systems because judges normally follow precedent, that is, the rules established in their own previous decisions, but they also have the power to change these rules when they do not fit the situation presented in court.

European civil law achieves continuity and flexibility in a different way. The written law sets forth principles and rules designed to cover all situations that come before the courts. The judges do not have the power to change these principles and rules, but they are expected to be flexible in interpreting and applying them. In that fashion, the written law can be adapted to the human needs in the unique situations before the courts. The judges are expected to respect the spirit, rather than the letter of the law.

Since Church or canon law more closely resembles European civil law, Church officials like bishops or pastors should not treat it in the way our American culture and tradition deals with written or statutory law, that is, by looking to the letter, rather than the spirit. Instead, they need to recognize that all law requires flexibility, as well as consistency. European and Church law achieve the flexibility necessary to adapt law to human needs and circumstances by entrusting that task to the one applying the law — the bishop or pastor in the case of Church law — who is expected to look to the spirit rather than the letter.

We could cite as an illustration of the need for flexibility and continuity in law the imaginary statute invented by the English legal philosopher H.L.A. Hart, which prohibited vehicles in the park.[37]

Imagine that a town council passed a statute making it a crime to bring vehicles into the park. Imagine also a justice of the peace responding to the many charges made by an overly conscientious police officer who arrests various people for using what the officer believes are vehicles in the park Should the justice of the peace find that bicycles, roller skates, baby carriages, toy trucks in the sand box, motorized wheel chairs, an ambulance rescuing a heart attack victim, and a police car racing into the park to interrupt a mugging are all vehicles prohibited in the park by the statute? In deciding these cases, should the judge look to the spirit of the statute (a desire to protect the safety and recreational uses of the park), or to the letter? Isn't the overly conscientious police officer guilty of looking at the letter, rather than the spirit of the law, and of failing to use common sense?

The Anglo-American or common law system prevails in countries among the western nations where English is the dominant language. That, of course, includes the United States and Canada. The European or civil law system prevails where the dominant language is one of the derivatives of Latin, but it also exists in other countries such as Germany, Russia, Holland, Austria and Japan. The state of Louisiana, however, is an exception, following the European or civil law.

Ramifications for American Catholics

All of this has practical ramifications for us as Catholics living in America. We inherit and imbibe the Anglo-American system of law. That means we are inclined to manifest great and sometimes an almost exaggerated respect for the law. Moreover, we also disdain those who seek exceptions or exemptions, we expect legislation to cover every aspect of life, and we normally do not violate even lesser civil regulations without inner anxiety. I offer two personal illustrations of the last point.

On a hot summer evening after speaking at a parish meeting in a small village 90 miles from my residence, I began the drive home. I halted at the town's only stoplight, observed no cars coming and turned right (generally legal in New York State, although I failed to observe the small sign there indicating in this case "No Turn on Red"). A few hundred yards up the road, a vehicle was creeping along ahead of me at a pace far below the posted rate. I passed the slow-moving automobile within the speed range allowed, but because of the darkness did not notice the solid double line down the road's center. A few minutes later the noise of a siren and the sight of flashing red lights in my mirror told me I was in trouble. I was not aware of any law violation, but instantly my heart started to pound, my breathing became labored and I felt like I had committed some unknown serious sin. Readers can judge whether or not my emotional and initial response was typical of Americans who willingly or otherwise violate the law.

The second illustration occurs frequently when I return from emergency calls in the middle of the night. I often stop on such occasions at the red light in intersections when no other car is anywhere in sight. Most Americans in that same situation would, I believe, hesitate to ignore the signal and drive through it or, if they did continue on, would feel some qualms.

Laws, therefore, are sacred for us. We do not lightly disobey or disregard them.

Nevertheless, canon law has been constructed according to the European or Roman, not the English or Anglo-American legal system. Interpreting Church law from the English or Anglo-American viewpoint tends to surround canon law of Church regulations with an inappropriate rigidity. Furthermore, it usually accepts, only with reluctance, the exceptions or applications which are an essential part of all European or Roman law. But Church law should not be perceived as a set of negative prohibitions like criminal law. On the contrary, it needs to be seen as having the basic goal or purpose of cultivating the ongoing, lifelong conversion process, rather than cursing prohibited actions.

Conclusion

The Church's legal system, therefore, offers many ways to demonstrate compassion and mercy — through its wide variety of laws, through its different exceptions or exemptions and through its interpretation or application of existing legislation to particular cases. At the same time, it insists that these deviations from the law not be done lightly or without proportionate reason. Church laws preserve the principle of consistency and truth, protect Church unity and concord and promote a desired spiritual communion among Catholics throughout the world. Too easy departure from the law undercuts all of those good effects.

Pastoral leaders, especially the clergy, thus must serve, in a sense, as informed and benign judges within the Church's legal system. Following the example of judges in the European tradition of law which we have described above, they must be aware of the law and its importance, but remain equally conscious of the law's limitations and the need for a wise, gentle application to individual cases. Furthermore, following that same parallel, they should remember that "the letter brings death, but the Spirit gives life" (2 Cor 3:6).

Let us apply our lengthy discussion about various legal systems and the role of judges in each to the case which began this chapter.

The old monsignor strictly interpreted canon 874 and applied the letter of that law to the situation before him. The woman was, in his words, "living in sin," and therefore not leading a life in harmony with the faith and role to be undertaken.

The neighboring pastor likewise gave canon 519 a strict, letter of the law interpretation which justified his refusal to get involved.

The priest recommended by the nun who approved the cousin as a godparent and baptized the child could, on the other hand, find a sound juridical basis for his pastoral action.

He might have, for instance, interpreted canon 874 in a more benign way, judging that the spirit of the law was being fulfilled, even though the letter of that law prohibited persons married out of the Church from acting as sponsors. The essential purpose of regulations about godparents is to insure that they assist the parents in giving the baptized a Christian formation. The cousin had done that in many ways for her own children and certainly agreed to do that for her godchild.

Or, he could have looked to canons 872, 873, and 874, no. 2 as regulations which provide alternatives and interpretations legally allowing the cousin to act as a sponsor or a witness.

The priest, finally, may have had recourse to one of the Church's exceptions, adaptations or exemptions, such as *epieikeia*, to support on a legal basis his decision to baptize the infant with the cousin as sponsor.

A correct understanding of the clergy's role as judges who benignly interpret and apply Church regulations according to the European or Roman legal system should help us accept a diversity of pastoral interpretations and applications. Instead of expecting that all will decide cases in the same fashion, we must anticipate that different clergy will judge differently in different circumstances. The strict monsignor probably grew annoyed when he heard that another priest approved the cousin as godparent and baptized the child. A better response would be for him to rest at ease that he had followed clear Church norms in making his decision, but to accept the fact that this other clergyman had also properly observed Church law in coming to his judgment.

Sometimes one hears the clergy complain about such differences, with the expressed desire for a uniformity in handling cases. From all we have noted in this chapter, it should be clear that such an unbending, rigid and frozen approach does not fit the European, Roman model of law. Some clergy in their judicial role will stress the challenge of consistency and truth; others will apply the balm of compassion and mercy. Both approaches have legal foundations. We need to develop a more tolerant attitude to that quite acceptable fact of divergent judgments.

In subsequent chapters we will describe this twofold task of judicial consistency and compassion as it applies to baptism and marriage.

Guidance from the *Catechism*

Article 1696: "The way of Christ 'leads to life'; a contrary way 'leads
to destruction' (*Mt* 7:13; cf. *Dt* 30:15-20). The Gospel parable of the *two ways* remains ever present in the
catechesis of the Church; it shows the importance of
moral decisions for our salvation: 'There are two ways,
the one of life, the other of death; but between the two,
there is a great difference'" (*Didache* 1, 1; SCh 248,
140).

Article 1724: "The Decalogue, the Sermon on the Mount, and the
apostolic catechesis describe for us the paths that lead
to the Kingdom of heaven. Sustained by the grace of
the Holy Spirit, we tread them, step by step, by everyday acts. By the working of the Word of Christ, we
slowly bear fruit in the Church to the glory of God"
(cf. the parable of the sower: *Mt* 13:3-23).

Article 1787: "Man is sometimes confronted by situations that make
moral judgments less assured and decision difficult.
But he must always seriously seek what is right and
good and discern the will of God expressed in divine
law."

Article 1952: "There are different expressions of the moral law, all
of them interrelated: eternal law—the source, in God,
of all law; natural law; revealed law, comprising the
Old Law and the New Law, or Law of the Gospel;
finally, civil and ecclesiastical laws."

6   A Warm Welcome

*W*hen I was a teenager — almost 15 years ago — I was very angry at God and his dear Mother to whom I had prayed. They didn't make me pretty or clear up my skin or get me a boyfriend. I know this sounds silly, but that was my world then. I thought if God didn't do what I begged for then he didn't love me. So I decided not to love him either.

My parents drove me and my two sisters to church each Sunday and I dreaded it. I sat thinking about what I was going to do when I got home and never paid attention. The pastor was new and very quiet and unassuming. He was always smiling. He stood a bit hunched over and his face was patchy with dryness. He waited after Mass and said hello to everybody. He said hello to me! He smiled and asked how I was.

In the early seventies we dressed in long blue jean skirts and old clothes and our parents hated it. We were rebellious and difficult to live with, I'm sure, but the constant nagging and comparisons to "good" kids never seemed to change us, only harden our attitudes.

As time went on I found it hard not to listen to this kind pastor's words. The sermons seemed to rhyme and the words were poetry. I was amazed. I loved writing and filled my school notebooks with poetry. Now this gentle priest was speaking my language. I would go out of my way to say hello to him and bring something for him to bless.

There was a church tag sale one day and we both reached for a Mexican vest. It was huge and colorful and I thought it would look great with my long skirts. Father liked it too. He did not seem to mind the way I looked or dressed. He spoke to me the way he spoke to everyone — with kindness and respect.

My cold heart began to melt and each Sunday I looked forward to Mass and to hear Father's "poetry." I began to learn about the Lord and his love. I began to see myself the way God did and my anger began to fade. I felt so horrible to ever have been angry at God and began to love him greater than ever.

I used to ask my family how they liked the sermons and didn't they think the way the words rhymed was beautiful. They said the sermons were fine but they didn't rhyme. They heard no poetry.

Father was later transferred and died rather young. He seemed lonely a lot and ill. I never told him about the poetry, but I've never stopped thinking about him all these years.

I know the Lord worked through him in a gentle but strong way. Sometimes now when I'm trying to convince my husband who refuses to go to Mass to join me, I think back to the manner Father used. He accepted me as I was. He didn't try to change me in a negative, commanding way, but change I did.   — *Connecticut*

I find it remarkable and encouraging that this kind and gentle pastor exerted such a positive and transforming influence upon the teenager from Connecticut. Her recollections over 15 years later are quite precise — the priest was very quiet and unassuming, his posture hunched over and his face patchy with dryness. Yet she apparently knew him only through rather surface connections — brief contacts at Masses or festivals and distant weekly absorption of his pulpit message from her place in the pews. Still the pastor's presence, approach and preaching touched her heart and changed her attitude.

If such almost routine interactions between clergy and parishioners have that kind of potential for positive transformations, how much greater are the possibilities for good when couples approach the parish offices seeking baptism or marriage. These are not surface exchanges, but meetings of moment; the couples are not distant observers, but persons vitally concerned about the outcome of this visit; they are usually not overly calm or emotionally aloof, but often feel awkward and apprehensive. The importance, involvement and intensity connected with the first session makes the initial interview a high-risk event indeed.

The high-risk factor caused by so many conscious and unconscious elements means that an encounter which goes well can touch the couple's hearts positively and change their attitudes significantly. Alas, the converse holds true. If the exchange goes badly, it can affect the pair negatively and seriously sour their feelings or judgments about the Church.

While we are centering here on the meetings linked with baptism and matrimony, the same observations hold true, even if to a somewhat lesser extent, for sessions connected with first penance, first Eucharist and confirmation. It should be obvious that high-risk encounters also occur on other occasions, like requests for anointing or care of the sick and for Christian burial.

Conscious and Unconscious Background Factors

It might be useful to reflect upon those conscious and unconscious elements which parents or engaged couples carry with them when they ask for the sacrament of baptism or wish to arrange for marriage in the Church. In the interest of simplicity we will examine those items as they pertain to the pair seeking matrimony; they apply as well with minor adjustments, but perhaps less force to parents who wish to have their children baptized.

1. *Awkwardness caused by unfamiliarity.* For many and probably most couples, arranging a personal interview with a member of the Catholic clergy and sitting down alone with him will be a first ever experience. All that accompanies such an event thus is unexplored territory. Questions like the following dominate their thinking: How do we contact him? Where do we meet? What do we say? How do we dress? What will he say?

Few people are totally comfortable with the unfamiliar. Probably the majority of persons, including those quite sophisticated, feel at least unsettled in these circumstances and some individuals may even be rather overwhelmed by the event.

2. *Mistrust or resentment.* Some scholars speculate that today many of our youth possess a hidden or perhaps overt attitude of mistrust and resentment toward all authority.

Part of that could be due to society's separation of the nurturing and disciplining roles of parents. As a consequence, children, according to these thinkers, are less able to integrate their sexual and aggressive instincts, thereby developing a mistrust of structures and a prejudice against religious ritual.[1]

Related to that development is the narcissism of our society with its consequent discrediting of authority in the home and classroom (as well as in the church).[2]

If these scholars have analyzed the contemporary culture correctly, then couples coming for marriage may bring along a certain subtle or maybe not so reserved resistance to structures, ritual and authority. The clergy clearly will personify for the engaged pair all three of those mistrusted or resented elements.

3. *Anxiety heightened by unusual circumstances.* When the couple bring with them any unusual problems, circumstances or requests, the level of anxiety normally rises.

Some of the more common examples of these are: if one or both have been previously married and are divorced, if they are already cohabiting, if either or both have slipped from faithful church attendance, if one is not Roman Catholic, if the bride-to-be is pregnant, if they wish something unique or special like being married in another location (e.g., in the bride's own Protestant church or at a neutral site such as the local hotel because one spouse is Jewish) or having a clergy friend from outside witness the vows.

In such situations they may nervously ask themselves beforehand: Will we be turned down because of the divorce(s)? Will he reprimand or reject us? Will my partner who is not Catholic like the priest or deacon? Will the pregnancy make a difference? Will he grant our requests and go along with our wishes?

4. *Attitudes caused by past burdens or blessings.* In his Apostolic Exhortation, *The Christian Family in the Modern World,* Pope John Paul II enlarged our vision of marriage preparation. He said that it is a gradual and continuous process embracing remote, proximate and immediate segments.[3] It includes not simply the formal classes or programs we associate with marital preparation, but family and environmental factors from the earliest childhood. These influences can, of course, be positive or negative, helpful or hurtful, constructive or destructive, blessings or burdens. In other words, all individuals are constantly being prepared, for better or for worse, for a possible future married life from the first moment of their existence in this world.

When either or both of the persons seeking marriage carry bad past baggage, when the family or environmental facts were burdens rather than blessings, the attitudes engendered by those experiences can jeopardize their future or jaundice their view of matrimony.

A few contemporary illustrations should make this evident.

• The high incidence of *marital disruptions.* There has been a slight decline in the number of divorces in the United States, but the totals and percentages remain astronomically high. Consider that divorces increased only gradually, although steadily, from 1860 through the early 1950's. Then the rate of divorces more than doubled over the next several decades. Almost half of the 1973 marriages ended in divorce as opposed to the 5 percent of the marriages in 1860 which terminated in divorce.[4] The divorce rate per 1,000 population in 1992 was 4.8; in 1994, 4.6; and in 1999, 4.2.

In 1999 there were 2,256,000 marriages and 1,141,590 divorces, still far too high.[5]

Almost half of today's children will spend some time in a single parent family, and for those whose mothers remarry about half will experience yet another family disruption as a child, since 40% of second marriages end in redivorce.[6]

The effects of such disruptions are still relatively unknown, but it should be evident that couples planning to marry can bear some serious scars upon them as a result of parental divorce and remarriage.

Of special significance is the indication that very young boys and girls often, on the conscious or unconscious levels, assume responsibility for the marital disruption. Irrational as this may be, it can still have a long-term harmful impact upon a child's self-image and cause continual complications later in life.

In a well-publicized case illustrative of this tendency, the central character recalls blaming herself during childhood as the cause of her parents' troubles. She remembers even telling her Cuddly Duddly, "It's all my fault my daddy and mommy don't like each other anymore."[7] That irrational acceptance of blame created serious difficulties in her own development both as a child and as an adolescent. It also overflowed into the early years of her marriage.

• *Abandonment, adoption and alcoholism.* Our growing modern awareness of the disease we call alcoholism gained through such groups as Alcoholics Anonymous and Adult Children of Alcoholics has made us aware of the sickness' effect upon not only the recovering alcoholic but also on all those, especially family members, who connect with the alcoholic person.

Abandonment and adoption are not as common or as publicized as alcoholism, but they, too, have the potential for creating inner difficulties throughout both the growing up and adult years.

Former U.S. Representative from Maryland, Robert Bauman, in a poignant autobiography, details how abandonment, adoption and alcoholism contributed to serious subsequent conflicts in his own life. Self-doubt, loneliness, low self-esteem and guilt about his sexuality fostered within him a drunkenness that ultimately became destructive. These led eventually to addictive drinking, a search for reassurance along unhealthy avenues, the break up of his marriage, the loss of his seat in Congress and periods of depression.[8]

These are but several of the many family and environmental factors which couples may bring as burdens when they seek marriage in the Church. Very frequently those negative influences either lurk underneath the surface or remain buried deep within the subconscious. In any event, whether open and obvious or hidden and obscure, they are powerful elements destined to affect the engaged pair's future together.

It is for the clergy simply to recognize the possibility of these potent forces being present within the man and woman who wish to marry.

5. *Preoccupation with external details.* The clergy and the couple very likely will be concerned about quite different matters during the initial meeting.

The clergy, comfortable with the familiar routine of arranging details for a marriage and perhaps struggling with the boredom of a task done so often, tend to be thinking about the couple's religious status, relationship with each other and attitude toward the sacrament of matrimony.

The engaged pair, on the other hand, probably will be more concerned about the practical details of the wedding. With today's difficulties in reserving a suitable place for the reception, their primary questions could be: Will we get the church for the date and time desired? After that, their preoccupation will usually center on externals such as: How do we contact the organist? Who will officiate? What are the costs? Where do we get the license? Must we attend classes? Is there a great deal of complicated paperwork?

Until these questioning concerns about the pragmatic details of the wedding are answered and the attending anxiety relieved, the engaged pair will not hear much that is said to them about relationships and religion.

6. *Uncomfortableness with a new relationship.* In addition to all the above factors, there exists the basic complexity of any three persons suddenly entering into a new relationship, in this case the couple and the priest or deacon. Sometimes the mix works immediately and well; at other times, the combinations involved do not blend so comfortably. There can be times when the chemistry among the three is instant and agreeable; at other times there may be personality clashes or temporary misunderstandings which leave all three uneasy.

Normally when strangers first meet there is a certain uncomfortableness as they break through outer barriers, learn about one another and gradually develop a mutual trust which will sustain or deepen the new relationship.

Developing a cordial relationship in a relatively brief period of time will take energy, skill and willingness on the part of the priest or deacon. But even with the best of intentions, the clergy cannot expect that a warm, caring and close bond will emerge with every couple who seeks to marry in the Church. As a popular contemporary author has observed, "There are flaws in every human connection."[9] But at least efforts can be expended to make the couple as comfortable as possible, to be gracious with them and to provide them the information or assistance they need.

To recognize that in all probability even the most sophisticated couple will feel at the initial session some uncomfortableness about entering into this new relationship could be the most essential step in establishing a cordial connection from the start.

Questions for the Clergy

Dominican David K. O'Rourke has already appeared twice in these pages, once in connection with the process called conversion and once in connection with our discussion about the "messy" as opposed to the "elitist" Church. He also has insightful things to say about the clergy who work with couples seeking marriage. O'Rourke possesses excellent credentials for making such assertions. Former pastor and Family Life director, he also edited the newsletter of diocesan family life directors and for that group coordinated a study of marriage preparation in American Catholic dioceses.[10]

In an article "Unfair Assessments: Obstacles for Engaged Couples," O'Rourke questions whether the clergy's concern today about Mass attendance as a prerequisite for a Church marriage may actually be more of an issue about power and authority. The church building and worship services could be seen as the clergy's turf. Their insistence upon weekly participation in the Eucharist by the engaged couple as a condition for a nuptial celebration thus might be an unconscious attempt to exert control over this area.[11]

That is interesting speculation. When we hear of clergy who display intense anger over a Catholic's marginal practice of the faith or who appear overly preoccupied with the parents' readiness for their infant's baptism or who grow unduly anxious about a couple's suitableness for marriage, one does wonder if there is not something more going on inside the priest or deacon than pure religious zeal.

The following questions may be useful for the clergy or other pastoral leaders in evaluating their own reactions and responses to the people who come to them for baptism, marriage and the other sacraments or simply for advice and support.

1. Do I have a need to be in control of all situations? How does this impact on my work with individuals who view religion and the Church differently from the way I view them?
2. When I am dealing with a couple who do not meet my expectations of spirituality and/or Mass attendance, does my need to be in control get in the way of my pastoral practice?
3. When I deal with individuals who are not practicing their faith as I feel that they should, do I immediately create an adversarial situation: me against them? Do I create a conflict that need not be and then become aggressive and overpowering?
4. Do I mistrust individuals who are not practicing Catholics before I even get to know them?

5. When I work with individuals who are indifferent to my values as a priest, does this engender in me feelings of abandonment?

6. Why do I find myself getting so angry when I work with Catholics who do not meet my expectations? Do I take it as a personal assault against my value system? When I sense that they are rejecting the Church, do I feel personally rejected and abandoned?

7. Is the anger that I am feeling toward this individual or couple appropriate, or is there something else happening inside me that causes me to displace my anger on them?

8. Do I feel victimized, used, or manipulated by couples who don't practice the faith but want a Church wedding? Where does this come from? Is my self-esteem too tied into the acceptance or rejection of the institution? Is it a question of wanting to be in control? Is it a question of rejection?

9. What feeling(s) does this particular situation, couple or family engender in me? Is it coming from them or am I projecting my issues onto them?

10. What effect does the pressure of ministry or priesthood have upon how I relate to individuals?

11. Am I feeling burned out or pressured? Do I consequently displace my feelings onto these people? Am I actually victimizing them because of my hurts and disappointments?

12. What are my expectations from this couple or individual? Am I hoping that they will fulfill or meet my needs? What are those needs?

13. Do I dread dealing with couples preparing for marriage? If so, what is going on inside me?

14. Am I always angry when the phone rings and it is another couple for marriage preparation? Where is this anger coming from? Am I overworked?

15. Do I feel overly responsible for how this individual or couple lives out their faith? Where does this come from?

16. What is my concept of Church? Is it a community of individu-

als who have it all together, who see things as I do, who meet all institutional expectations? If this is so, won't my ministry always be frustrated?[12]

Two contemporary writers offer us some guidance on these subtle and often subliminal matters of control, over-responsibility, conflict or aggressiveness, abandonment and expectations.

On *control*:

Control is perhaps the most dominant issue in our lives. No matter what we think we have to control, whether someone else's behavior, our own behavior or something else, our codependent self tends to latch on to this notion and won't let go. The result is often suffering, confusion and frustration.

On *over-responsibility*:

Many of us who grew up in troubled or dysfunctional families learned to become overly responsible. That often seemed the only way to avoid many of our painful feelings, such as anger, fear and hurt. It also gave us the illusion of being in control.

On *conflict and aggressiveness*:

Growing up in a troubled or dysfunctional family, we learn to avoid conflict whenever possible. When conflict occurs, we learn mostly to withdraw from it in some way. Occasionally, we become aggressive and try to overpower those with whom we are in conflict.

On *abandonment*:

Fear of being abandoned goes all the way back to our earliest seconds, minutes and hours of existence. Related to the issue of trust and distrust, it is often exaggerated among children who grew up in troubled or dysfunctional families.[13]

On *expectations:*

I've learned that in the course of our life we leave and are left and let go of much that we love. Losing is the price we pay for living. It is also the source of much of our growth and gain. Making our way from birth to death, we also have to make our way through the pain of giving up and giving up and giving up some portion of what we cherish…. And in giving up our impossible expectations, we become a lovingly connected self, renouncing ideal visions of perfect friendship, marriage, children, family life for the sweet imperfections of all-too-human relationships.[14]

The clergy and other pastoral leaders would surely accept the position that they are called to be loving servants of others, giving themselves in and with Christ's love for others. But love means accepting people as they are, not as we want them to be and not as they ought to be. This requires that we grasp the sometimes hard to take truths that there are flaws in every human connection, that in ourselves and in other people there is the mingling of love with hate, of the good with the bad, that what hurts us cannot always be kissed and made better, that we are utterly powerless to offer ourselves or others total protection from danger and pain, from the inroads of time, from the coming of age and the coming of death. There are universal, unavoidable and inexorable losses.[15]

We mentioned that individuals who come to the clergy bring the burdens and blessings of who they are and where they come from to those encounters. But the clergy and pastoral leaders do the same. Their own attitudes are greatly affected by family influences and environmental factors. For this reason it is highly desirable for the clergy through personal reflection and perhaps professional therapy to understand more thoroughly their own background burdens and blessings which can impact the way they look at, speak to and interact with others.

Practical Suggestions

In a later chapter specifically dealing with pastoral suggestions for marriage, I will offer a series of non-threatening questions for the initial interview between the priest or deacon and the engaged pair. They have been employed for many years with countless couples as a means of breaking down barriers, of reducing that high-risk nature of the first session and of extending to the prospective bride and groom a warm welcome.

What follows below are general recommendations applicable to any first exchange between the clergy or pastoral leaders and those who seek the sacraments or other official services of the parish:

1. *Personal, not telephone or written interviews.* Our own experiences in life have taught us how telephone exchanges or printed correspondence can easily cause misunderstandings. Moreover, we may say harsh things over the telephone or write hard things in a letter which would be softened, clarified or omitted if we were communicating face to face.

Counseling and communication expert Patricia Livingston cites some statistics which give a theoretical basis to these experiential observations. According to her studies, 55 percent of communication happens by visual means or by appearances. Folded arms and glances at one's watch convey one message; a broad smile and an erect, but relaxed posture convey something quite the opposite. The eyes, we have been told, are doorways to the soul.

Those same statistics indicate 38 percent of communication occurs through the tone of one's voice. Identical words can convey very different meanings depending upon the way we speak them.

Only seven percent of communication, according to Livingston, happens because of the actual content of the message itself.

The potential for misunderstanding and harm through a telephone exchange is so great and the possibility for communication and good through a personal interview is so enormous that we strongly urge the latter. In that situation we can see the others' faces, sense their feelings and catch the meaning behind the words spoken.

When Church personnel discuss baptism, marriage or similar matters in detail over the telephone with the interested parties, they tread a perilous path. The risks involved in such an approach are staggering. They would be better advised simply to listen carefully over the telephone, exude loving warmth, offer no judgments or answers and request that, whatever the context, the callers come to the office where these always delicate matters can be discussed more fully and satisfactorily. The telephone exchange, then, merely identifies the issue, creates an initial positive atmosphere and arranges a future personal appointment.

2. *Avoid defensiveness.* Many of those who come seeking the sacraments will, in our day, hold certain values or follow some practices contrary to the teaching of the Church. This can trigger negative reactions in the clergy or pastoral leaders if they view them as personal attacks or make judgments about the people's individual culpability in these matters. Such defensiveness causes inner anguish for the clergy or parish leaders and at the same time diminishes their own pastoral effectiveness. The leaders need, of course, to uphold the Church's teachings and challenge people to be more. But in accomplishing this task, they would do well to keep in mind the words of Pope Paul VI. He urged pastoral ministers to imitate Jesus who was "indeed intransigent with evil, but merciful toward individuals."[16]

The questions we posed above for the clergy and pastoral leaders speak to this point of defensiveness.

3. *Be positive and flexible.* Even if there are present several complications and negative factors, those who come to the Church for sacraments or services usually do so with good will. Moreover, these contacts with the Church often are prompted by events of joy and hope, whether it be the birth of a child or the love between a couple.

It is for the clergy and pastoral leaders to respond to such expressions of good will, joy and hope in positive ways by congratulating the callers, praising them and rejoicing with them over their recent blessing. To welcome them warmly, to thank them for their confidence and to offer them an explanation with some enthusiasm for what the Church has to offer starts the first encounter off in the right direction and augurs well for future exchanges.

While diocesan or parish norms or guidelines are necessary and good, the clergy and pastoral leaders need an open, flexible frame of mind in responding to the circumstances of those who come to them. Essential preparation and requirements naturally must be cared for, but the accidental can and should be adjusted. We would hope to see a minimum of arbitrary tests or negative rules on the parish level.

The letters introducing chapters of this book give ample testimony of the hurts which happen when leaders inflexibly insist upon accidental or incidental requisites. The previous chapter indicated how flexible in fact are Church laws, admitting rather easily of adaptation and application.

4. *No interruptions.* When the clergy or pastoral ministers interrupt an interview with a telephone call or a temporary exit from the meeting room, the person(s) may well begin to feel uncomfortable, neglected, unimportant and annoyed.

I would urge as a principle that no telephone interruptions be attempted or accepted during interviews with the exception of emergency messages or long-distance calls.

Evangelization

During the year of research in preparation for writing this book, I directed workshops for the clergy in some half-dozen dioceses of the United States and Canada. As part of those conferences we discussed pastoral approaches to marginal Catholics in light of the principles in this book. The exchanges were always animated and sometimes rather heated.

I have heard responses like these:

"I have never wanted to be a cop or an enforcer in the Church, but was beginning to question if I must start to be one in connection with the sacraments. After our discussions, I am very much relieved and reassured that my instinctive way of doing ministry was correct."

"I always considered these sacramental occasions as important catechetical opportunities. Now I see them more as movements for evangelization."

Pope Paul VI's Apostolic Exhortation *On Evangelization in the Modern World* provides some helpful guidance in viewing the sacraments as occasions for evangelizing participants.

He reminds us that the Church is in constant need of being evangelized herself. Since "she is the People of God immersed in the world, and often tempted by idols,... she always needs to be called together afresh by him...."[17]

The pope cites different kinds of marginal Catholics in special need of evangelization: those baptized, "but who live quite outside the Christian life"; "simple people who have a certain faith but an imperfect knowledge of the foundations of that faith"; "intellectuals who feel the need to know Jesus Christ in a light different from the instructions they received as children"; "a very large number of baptized people who for the most part have not formally renewed their baptism but who are entirely indifferent to it and not living in accordance with it" (sec. 52; 56).

Pope Paul VI offers an explanation behind the existence of marginal Catholics: "The phenomenon of the non-practicing is a very ancient one in the history of Christianity; it is the result of a natural weakness, a profound inconsistency which we unfortunately bear deep within us. Today however it shows certain new characteristics. It is often the result of the uprooting typical of our time. It also springs from the fact that Christians live in close proximity with non-believers and constantly experience the effects of unbelief. Furthermore, the non-practicing Christians of today, more so than those of previous periods, seek to explain and justify their position in the name of an interior religion, of personal independence or authenticity" (sec. 56).

Finally, he reminds evangelizers that while it is the "gentle action of the Spirit" which brings about an "interior change," they themselves must be servants of the truth and animated by love (sec. 75; 18; 78-79). That double duty of truth and love echoes the balance of consistency and truth with compassion and mercy which has been the theme of this book.

The Holy Father speaks these words to evangelizers as servants of truth and consistency:

> Every evangelizer is expected to have a reverence for truth, especially since the truth that he studies and communicates is none other than revealed truth and hence, more than any other, a sharing in the first truth which is God himself. The preacher of the Gospel will therefore be a person who even at the price of personal renunciation and suffering always seeks the truth that he must transmit to others. He never betrays or hides truth out of a desire to please men, in order to astonish or to shock, nor for the sake of originality or a desire to make an impression. He does not refuse truth. He does not obscure revealed truth by being too idle to search for it, or for the sake of his own comfort, or out of fear. He does not neglect to study it. He serves it generously, without making it serve him (sec. 78).

Pope Paul VI addresses these balancing words to evangelizers as persons animated by love. Their love must be the love of a father and the love of a mother, more than that of a teacher. This kind of love manifests itself in two ways, among others:

> The first is respect for the religious and spiritual situation of those being evangelized. Respect for their tempo and pace; no one has the right to force them excessively. Respect for their conscience and convictions, which are not to be treated in a harsh manner.

Another sign of this love is concern not to wound the other person, especially if he or she is weak in faith, with statements that may be clear for those who are already initiated but which for the faithful can be a source of bewilderment and scandal, like a wound in the soul. (sec. 79).

Conclusion

Describing his high school years in *Lake Wobegon Days,* Garrison Keillor related how "worry ate at Mr. Detman," the principal. Fearful that students living in the country would be marooned and perish during a blizzard on their way home, Detman announced that each rural pupil would be assigned a "Storm Home" in the village.

Keillor imagined how the Kloeckls had personally chosen him as their storm child simply because they liked him. "In the event of a blizzard, we want that boy! The skinny one with the thick glasses!"

There were no blizzards that year, but the adolescent Keillor often thought of the Kloeckls and their little green cottage by the lake. They grew large in his imagination — his storm house.

Blizzards aren't the only storms and not the worst by any means. I could imagine worse things. If the worst should come, I could go to the Kloeckls and knock on their door. "Hello," I'd say. "I'm your storm child."

"Oh, I know," she'd say. "I was wondering when you'd come. Oh, it's good to see you. How would you like a hot chocolate and an oatmeal cookie?"

We'd sit at the table. "Looks like this storm is going to last awhile," she'd continue.

"Yes."

"But we're so glad to have you. I can't tell you. Carl! Come down and see who's here!"

"Is it the storm child?"

"Yes! Himself, in the flesh!"[18]

The people who come to our parishes seeking one of the sacraments or some other pastoral service are often persons caught in the storms of life. They may be spiritually lost or confused, cold or hungry, frightened or discouraged. They sometimes are not even sure of exactly what they want. But the Church seems for them to be a possible storm home; they hope to find there a safe refuge in the midst of their personal blizzards; they imagine receiving kind words, helpful advice and supportive nourishment from those who open the door.

But these wandering individuals understand all too well how long and how far they have been away from this home. They may worry that the door will be slammed in their faces or that eventually they will be rejected, turned away and cast back into the dreadful blizzard outside.

A warm welcome reassures callers that they have in fact rediscovered their true spiritual storm home and have finally returned to the house of God where they belong.

Guidance from the *Catechism*

Article 425: "The transmission of the Christian faith consists primarily in proclaiming Jesus Christ in order to lead others to faith in him. From the beginning, the first disciples burned with the desire to proclaim Christ: 'We cannot but speak of what we have seen and heard' (*Acts* 4:20). And they invite people of every era to enter into the joy of their communion with Christ...."

Article 2226: "The parish is the Eucharistic community and the heart of the liturgical life of Christian families; it is a privileged place for the catechesis of children and parents."

Article 160: "To be human, 'man's response to God by faith must be free, and... therefore nobody is to be forced to embrace the faith against his will. The act of faith is of its very nature a free act' (*DH* 10; cf. CIC, can. 748 §2). 'God calls men to serve him in spirit and in truth. Consequently they are bound to him in conscience, but not coerced.... This fact received its fullest manifestation in Christ Jesus' (*DH* 11). Indeed, Christ invited people to faith and conversion, but never coerced them. 'For he bore witness to the truth but refused to use force to impose it on those who spoke against it. His kingdom... grows by the love with which Christ, lifted up on the cross, draws men to himself'" (*DH* 11; cf. *Jn* 18:37; 12:32).

Article 1550: "This presence of Christ in the minister is not to be understood as if the latter were preserved from all human weaknesses, the spirit of domination, error, even sin. The power of the Holy Spirit does not guarantee all acts of ministers in the same way. While this guarantee extends to the sacraments, so that even the minister's sin cannot impede the fruit of grace, in many other acts the minister leaves human traces that are not always signs of fidelity to the Gospel and consequently can harm the apostolic fruitfulness of the Church."

7 Baptism: Official Directives

*A*s a permanent deacon I have a "balancing" problem in administering the sacraments.

Of great concern to me as a high school teacher is the welfare of unwed teenage parents and their children. My most recent example is a friend of my daughter. She is 18 with a two-year-old child.

The young woman's father was shot to death 15 years ago and her mother died two years ago. She and her daughter live alone and receive financial assistance from social security. She gets emotional support from friends, grandparents, teachers, and some of her sisters. She will graduate from high school in a couple of months, at which time her social security will run out, but she sees a need to continue her education.

The father of the child is Catholic, as were her own parents, although it appears marginally so. She would like a Catholic baptism for her daughter, but she is not baptized.

My response to her was that it really wouldn't make much sense to baptize her daughter if she herself were not baptized. I encouraged her to receive instruction for herself, which would help her in the child's formation as well as provide a strong rationale for baptizing the child.

Now that I have said it, it doesn't seem right for the circumstances. It sounds too much like bargaining for sacraments. It now appears to me that her child's baptism could be a source of strength and renewal ("a moment of grace") for this young mother which would lead her to her own profession of faith.

I would also like to investigate the relationship with the father of the child, since he appears to be somewhat active in the child's life.

This, my balancing act story, is not simple, but it doesn't seem so odd, either.   — *Minnesota*

The next two chapters, as the titles indicate, deal specifically with baptism, first from a legal and official viewpoint and then from a practical and pastoral perspective.

This chapter will be somewhat technical. It presents the authentic teaching of the Catholic Church on baptism as found in three Vatican documents: the *Rite of Baptism for Children* published in 1969, the *Instruction on Infant Baptism* issued by the Sacred Congregation for the Doctrine of the Faith in Vatican City, October 20, 1980, and the 1983 *Code of Canon Law*.

All offer general guidelines and even some precise norms, but, as we will see, they leave ultimate decisions about a particular baptism to the local parish clergy.

Rite of Baptism for Children

The Introduction to this ritual begins by speaking about the baptism of infants and their subsequent Christian formation. It declares that the baptism of infants is important, necessary and has been the practice of the Church from the earliest times. Once baptized, however, children must be formed in the faith. That faith is not the private faith of the individual or family. Instead it is the faith of the Church in its entirety, both of the local Christian community and of the whole society of believers.

From the earliest times, the Church, to which the mission of preaching the gospel and of baptizing was entrusted, has baptized children as well as adults. Our Lord said: "Unless a man is reborn in water and the Holy Spirit, he cannot enter the kingdom of God." The Church has always understood these words to mean that children should not be deprived of baptism, because they are baptized in the faith of the Church. This faith is proclaimed for them by their parents and godparents, who represent both the local church and the whole society of saints and believers: "The Church is at once the mother of all and the mother of each" (no. 2).

To fulfill the true meaning of the sacrament, children must later be formed in the faith in which they have been baptized. The foundation of this formation will be the sacrament itself, which they have already received. Christian formation, which is their due, seeks to lead them gradually to learn God's plan in Christ, so that they may ultimately accept for themselves the faith in which they have been baptized (no. 3).

In this way it is clear that the faith in which the children are baptized is not the private possession of the individual family, but it is the common treasure of the whole Church of Christ (no. 4).

After explaining the function of the people of God, the Church made present in the local community in the baptism and Christian formation of both children and adults, the ritual details the role of parents in these tasks. Their ministry in baptism is more important than that of godparents. Moreover, they should be present and actively participate in the liturgical celebration itself (no. 4; 5:2-3).

Preparation of the parents' minds and hearts for the baptismal celebration and later Christian formation is of crucial importance.

Before the celebration of the sacrament, it is of great importance that parents, moved by their own faith or with the help of friends or other members of the community, should prepare to take part in the rite with understanding. They should be provided with suitable means such as books, instructions, and catechisms written for families. The parish priest should make it his duty to visit them, or see that they are visited, as a family or as a group of families, and prepare them for the coming celebration by pastoral counsel and common prayer (no. 5:1).

After baptism it is the responsibility of the parents, in their gratitude to God and in fidelity to the duty they have undertaken, to enable the child to know God, whose adopted child it has become, to receive confirmation, and to participate in the holy Eucharist. In this duty they are again to be helped by the parish priest by suitable means (no. 5:5).

The Introduction also mentions the situation in which one of the parents cannot make the profession of faith during the liturgy of baptism. It goes on to comment about that person's responsibilities, an observation which relates closely to an earlier case we cited. In that instance the father who was not Catholic agreed that his wife could bring up the children in the faith, but he would not come to the mandated classes.

If one of the parents cannot make the profession of faith (if, for example, he is not a Catholic), he may keep silent. All that is asked of him, when he requests baptism for the child, is that he should make arrangements, or at least give permission, for the child to be instructed in the faith of its baptism (no. 5:4).

Under a section outlining the time for the baptism of children, the ritual addresses those delicate issues involving marginal Catholics which we are examining in this book. The following paragraphs should be read carefully because the concepts in them will be repeated and expanded in the other documents which were published more than a decade later.

As for the time of baptism, the first consideration is the welfare of the child, that it may not be deprived of the benefit of the sacrament; then the health of the mother must be considered, so that as far as possible she too may be present. Then, as long as they do not interfere with the greater good of the child, there are pastoral considerations such as allowing sufficient time to prepare the parents and for planning the actual celebration to bring out its paschal character (no. 8).

As soon as possible and even before the child is born, the parents should be in touch with the parish priest concerning the baptism, so that proper preparation may be made for the celebration (no. 8:2).

An infant should be baptized within the first weeks after birth. The conference of bishops may, for sufficiently serious pastoral reasons, determine a longer interval of time between birth and baptism (no. 8:3).

When the parents are not yet prepared to profess the faith or to undertake the duty of bringing up their children as Christians, it is for the parish priest, keeping in mind whatever regulations may have been laid down by the conference of bishops, to determine the time for the baptism of infants (no. 8:4).

Certain quite particular norms for the place or setting of the baptismal liturgy also include further insights about the nature of faith and the implication of baptism.

To bring out the paschal character of baptism, it is recommended that the sacrament be celebrated during the Easter Vigil or on Sunday, when the Church commemorates the Lord's resurrection. On Sunday, baptism may be celebrated even during Mass, so that the entire community may be present and the necessary relationship between baptism and Eucharist may be clearly seen, but this should not be done too often (no. 9).

So that baptism may clearly appear as the sacrament

of the Church's faith and of admittance into the people of God, it should normally be celebrated in the parish church, which must have a baptismal font (no. 10).

The Introduction also suggests that conferences of bishops may issue pastoral directives to deal with circumstances in which a significant number of children will fail to receive a Christian education and may even lose the faith. Our National Conference of Catholic Bishops has not acted upon this suggestion and we thus have no such guidelines for parish priests and deacons.

In many countries parents are sometimes not ready for the celebration of baptism or they ask for their children to be baptized, although the latter will not afterwards receive a Christian education and will even lose the faith. Since it is not enough to instruct the parents and to inquire about their faith in the course of the rite itself, conferences of bishops may issue pastoral directives, for the guidance of parish priests, to determine a longer interval between birth and baptism (no. 25).

The rite, finally, has a word to say about the content and tone of baptismal preparation meetings.

During meetings to prepare the parents for the baptism of their children, it is important that the instruction should be supported by prayer and religious rites. The various elements provided in the rite of baptism for the celebration of the word of God will prove helpful (no. 27).

Instruction on Infant Baptism

In 1980 the Sacred Congregation for the Doctrine of the Faith issued an Instruction as a response to some of the practices and problems connected with infant baptism since the Second Vatican

Council. "Many parents," it reads, "are distressed to see their children abandoning the faith and no longer receiving the sacraments, in spite of their own efforts to give them a Christian upbringing, and some pastors are asking themselves whether they should not be stricter before admitting infants to baptism" (no. 2). In reaction to these trends, it continues, there are those who have proposed a new policy eliminating infant baptism and postponing the sacrament until "such an age when an individual can make a personal commitment, perhaps even until the beginning of adult life," and this denial, refusal or delay of infant baptism has "scandalized many parents" (no. 2).

The text in response defends at length the traditional doctrine on infant baptism and then, in a second section, offers answers to several pertinent difficulties being raised in our day. Finally, part three provides some pastoral directives with regard to infant baptism. The last portion of that division is especially helpful in our consideration of marginally Catholic parents who seek baptism for their children.

The document, first of all, states that pastoral practice which touches upon infant baptism "must be governed by two great principles, the second of which is subordinate to the first."

1. Baptism, which is necessary for salvation, is the sign and the means of God's prevenient love, which frees us from original sin and communicates to us a share in divine life. Considered in itself, the gift of these blessings to infants must not be delayed.

2. Assurances must be given that the gift thus granted can grow by an authentic education in the faith and Christian life, in order to fulfill the true meaning of the sacrament. As a rule, these assurances are to be given by the parents or close relatives, although various substitutions are possible within the Christian community. But if these assurances are not really serious there can be grounds for delaying the sacrament; and if they are certainly non-existent the sacrament should even be refused (no. 28).

The Instruction then describes the need and thrust of a "pastoral dialogue between the priest and the family," recalling, but restating directives given in the Rite of Infant Baptism. We cited these in the preceding part of this chapter and add here the reformulated recommendations.

> In the first place, much importance is given to the presence and active participation of the parents in the celebration. The parents now have priority over the godparents, although the presence of the latter continues to be required, since their assistance in the child's education is valuable and can sometimes be essential.
>
> Secondly, preparation for the baptism has an important place. The parents must give thought to the baptism; they should inform their pastors of the coming birth and prepare themselves spiritually. The pastors, for their part, will visit the families or gather them together and give them catechesis and appropriate advice. They will also urge the families to pray for the children that they are expecting (no. 29).

With regard to the time of baptism, it quotes the norms of the ritual which notes three facts to be considered in determining the moment when to baptize a child: the welfare of the child, the benefit of the mother, and pastoral considerations "such as allowing sufficient time to prepare the parents and for planning the active celebration to bring out its paschal character" (no. 29).

As a rule, however, it states that an infant should be baptized within the first weeks after birth (no. 29).

This Vatican Instruction touches the heart of considerations in our book when it examines the "Dialogue between pastors and families with little faith or non-Christian families" (no. 30).

The text describes those situations in this way: "It sometimes happens that pastors are approached by parents who have little faith and practice their religion only occasionally, or even by non-Christian parents who request baptism for their children for reasons that deserve consideration" (no. 30).

Our pastoral response in such circumstances should be based on these three rules:

1. "In this case the pastor will endeavor by means of a clear-sighted and understanding dialogue to arouse the parents' interest in the sacrament they are requesting and make them aware of the responsibility that they are assuming" (no. 30).
2. "In fact the Church can only accede to the desire of these parents if they give an assurance that, once the child is baptized, it will be given the benefit of the Christian upbringing required by the sacrament. The Church must have a well-founded hope that the baptism will bear fruit" (no. 30).
3. "With regard to the assurances, any pledge giving a well-founded hope for the Christian upbringing of the children deserves to be considered as sufficient" (no. 31).

Once the clear-sighted and understanding dialogue is completed, the Instruction describes the action alternatives.

1. "If the assurances given — for example, the choice of godparents who will take sincere care of the child, or the support of the community of the faithful — are sufficient, the priest cannot refuse to celebrate the sacrament without delay, as in the case of children of Christian families" (no. 30).
2. "If on the other hand they are insufficient, it will be prudent to delay baptism. However the pastors should keep in contact with the parents so as to secure, if possible, the conditions required on their part for the celebration of the sacrament. If even this solution fails, it can be suggested, as a last recourse, that the child be enrolled in a catechumenate to be given when the child reaches school age" (no. 30).
3. "It must be clear that the refusal of baptism is not a means of exercising pressure. Nor can one speak of refusal, still less of discrimination, but rather of educational delay, according to individual cases, aimed at helping the family to grow in faith or to become more aware of its responsibilities" (no. 31).

4. "Enrollment for a future catechumenate should not be accompanied by a specially created rite which would easily be taken as an equivalent of the sacrament itself. It should also be clear that this enrollment is not admittance to the catechumenate and that the infants enrolled cannot be considered catechumens with all the prerogatives attached to being such. They must be presented later on for a catechumenate suited to their age. In this regard, it must be stated clearly that the existence in the Rite of Christian Initiation of Adults or a Rite of Initiation for Children of Catechetical Age in no way means that the Church considers it preferable or normal to delay baptism until that age" (no. 31).

5. "Finally, in areas where families of little faith or non-Christian families make up the majority, so as to justify the local setting up by the Bishop' Conference of a joint pastoral plan which provides for postponing baptism beyond the time fixed by the general law, Christian families living in these areas retain the full right to have their children baptized earlier. The sacrament is therefore to be administered in accordance with the Church's will and as the faith and generosity of these families deserve" (no. 31).

6. "It is important to intensify pastoral care of engaged couples at meetings in preparation for marriage, and likewise the pastoral care of young couples. The whole ecclesial community must be called upon as circumstances demand, especially teachers, married couples, family action movements, religious congregations and secular institutes. Priests must give this apostolate an important place in their ministry. In particular, they will remind parents of their responsibilities in awakening their children's faith and educating it. It is in fact for parents to begin the religious initiation of the child, to teach it to love Christ as a close friend and to form its conscience. This task will be all the more fruitful and easy if it builds on the grace of baptism present in the child's heart" (no. 32).

Code of Canon Law

The 1983 *Code of Canon Law* treats of baptism mainly in Book IV, "The Office of Sanctifying in the Church" under Title I, Canons 849-878. There are references to baptism in several other locations of the code, but the major legislation on this sacrament can be found under Title I.

As might be expected, the code incorporated the earlier directives of both the *Rite of Baptism for Children* and the *Instruction on Infant Baptism* within its own canons on baptism.

The following canons or sections of them are pertinent to our discussions in this book.

The parents of an infant who is to be baptized and likewise those who are to undertake the office of sponsor are to be properly instructed in the meaning of this sacrament and the obligations which are attached to it; personally or through others the pastor is to see to it that the parents are properly formed by pastoral directions and by common prayer, gathering several families together and where possible visiting them (canon 851:2).

Parents are obliged to see to it that infants are baptized within the first weeks after birth; as soon as possible after the birth or even before it parents are to go to the pastor to request the sacrament for their child and to be properly prepared for it (canon 867:1).

For the licit baptism of an infant it is necessary that:

1. the parents or at least one of them or the person who lawfully takes their place gives consent;
2. there be a founded hope that the infant will be brought up in the Catholic religion; if such a hope is altogether lacking, the baptism is to be put off according to the prescriptions of particular law and the parents are to be informed of the reason (canon 868:1).

Insofar as possible one to be baptized is to be given a

sponsor who is to assist an adult in Christian initiation, or, together with the parents, to present an infant at the baptism, and who will help the baptized to lead a Christian life in harmony with baptism, and to fulfill faithfully the obligations connected with it (canon 872).

Only one male or one female sponsor or one of each sex is to be employed (canon 873).

To be admitted to the role of sponsor, a person must:

1. be designated by the one to be baptized, by the parents or the one who takes their place or, in their absence, by the pastor or minister and is to have the qualifications and intention of performing this role;
2. have completed the sixteenth year, unless a different age has been established by the diocesan bishop or it seems to the pastor or minister that an exception is to be made for a just cause;
3. be a Catholic who has been confirmed and has already received the sacrament of the Most Holy Eucharist and leads a life in harmony with the faith and the role to be undertaken;
4. not be bound by any canonical penalty legitimately imposed or declared;
5. not be the father or the mother of the one to be baptized (canon 874:1).

A baptized person who belongs to a non-Catholic ecclesial community may not be admitted except as a witness to baptism and together with a Catholic sponsor (canon 874:2).

We will now attempt to tie together all the information presented in this and the preceding chapters by developing some practical, pragmatic or pastoral suggestions for ministering the sacrament of baptism to infants, including children of parents who by our definition are marginal Catholics.

Guidance from the *Catechism*

Article 1213: "Holy Baptism is the basis of the whole Christian life, the gateway to life in the Spirit (*vitae spiritualis ianua*) [Council of Florence: DS 1314: *vitae spiritualis ianua*], and the door which gives access to the other sacraments. Through Baptism we are freed from sin and reborn as sons of God; we become members of Christ, are incorporated into the Church and made sharers in her mission: 'Baptism is the sacrament of regeneration through water in the word'" (*Roman Catechism* II, 2, 5; cf. Council of Florence: DS 1314; CIC, can. 204 §1; 849; CCEO, can. 675 §1).

Article 1216: "Baptism is God's most beautiful and magnificent gift.... We call it gift, grace, anointing, enlightenment, garment of immortality, bath of rebirth, seal, and most precious gift. It is called *gift* because it is conferred on those who bring nothing of their own; *grace* since it is given even to the guilty; *Baptism* because sin is buried in the water; *anointing* for it is priestly and royal as are those who are anointed; *enlightenment* because it radiates light; *clothing* since it veils our shame; *bath* because it washes; and *seal* as it is our guard and the sign of God's Lordship" (St. Gregory of Nazianzus, *Oratio* 40, 3-4; PG 36, 361C).

Article 1229: From the time of the apostles, becoming a Christian has been accomplished by a journey and initiation in several stages. This journey can be covered rapidly or slowly, but certain essential elements will always have to be present: proclamation of the Word, acceptance of the Gospel entailing conversion, profession of faith, Baptism itself, the outpouring of the Holy Spirit, and admission to Eucharistic communion.

Article 1234: The meaning and grace of the sacrament of Baptism are clearly seen in the rites of its celebration. By following the gestures and words of this celebration with attentive participation, the faithful are initiated into the riches this sacrament signifies and actually brings about in each newly baptized person.

8 Baptism: Pastoral Suggestions

*W*e are writing this letter to say thank you to one of the priests there at St. Francis'. I hope you do not find this letter too strange. We'd like to share with you some very wonderful things that have happened to us. Toward the end of this letter you will realize why we are writing this.

We were married at St. Francis' in 1974. My husband was Catholic and I was Lutheran. Since our marriage, we've lived in Cheyenne, Wyoming; Riverside, California; and Presque Isle, Maine, where we presently live. We've moved around so much because my husband is in the Air Force. We have two children — Jarred, seven, and Kelly, four.

From 1974 through 1980, we never went to church. Frank wasn't practicing his faith, nor did I practice mine. We found out we were moving to Maine, and had to arrive by the end of November. We had been thinking of getting the children baptized for some time, but never did. Then the whole thing of fear started setting in, like "what if something happens to the children and they are not baptized?" With the thought of traveling across country, we wanted to get them baptized before we left.

So, Frank called St. Francis' and talked to a priest. He told him we were moving in two weeks and wanted to get our children baptized at St. Francis' where we were married. The priest asked if we were going to church and practicing our faith. Frank told him no, and the priest flatly refused to baptize our children. He told us we should find a church in Presque Isle and start going every Sunday, and then talk to a priest about baptism. To say the least, we were angry and hurt, and couldn't believe he turned us away.

Well, we moved to Presque Isle. About a month went by, and I was having terrible problems with anxiety. I had a lot of trouble with it in California also. One day it got so bad that I shut myself in my room and screamed and cried. I pounded on the bed and the wall. I was so afraid to face another day. I felt I couldn't take it any more. At that moment, I felt God talking to me, and I quieted down. It was like a voice coming from within. It spoke softly and said, "Lynn, don't carry this burden any longer. Give it to Christ. That is why He died for you. He will take this suffering from you." I prayed and begged him to do just that.

Soon after that happened, I was driving past St. Mary's church one morning on the way home from the store. I sat at the stoplight and watched all the people coming out of Mass. I saw the priest and heard his voice. I felt a good feeling come over me. I drove home and asked Frank if we could go to church next Sunday. He said he was thinking the same thing.

Sunday came, and we went to Mass. It felt good to Frank to be back in the Catholic Church again. For me, it was very scary, but I had a real sense of wanting to be there.

We went back the next Sunday sitting a little closer to the altar. The third Sunday we sat even closer. I really got involved in the Mass. I felt the prayers, I felt the music and such a calm came over me that I couldn't feel myself breathe. When it came to the offertory and preparing to celebrate the Eucharist, tears started pouring down my face and I couldn't stop them.

I realized at that moment what the Eucharist meant to me and just why the Mass was so centered around it. When Mass was over, I told Frank I wanted to become a Catholic and wanted to talk to the priest about it.

That week we had an appointment with our pastor. We talked about a lot of things — baptism for the children, confirmation for Frank, and entering the catechumenate for myself. The realization occurred to us that it was important for us, and to us and our children, that we go to Mass every Sunday and become faithful members of our parish and community. It meant we would have so much more to offer our children. We found a strong faith to share, a great love for God and the community.

In the ensuing months Frank and I grew stronger and closer. He went to classes and was confirmed in May of last year. I went through the RCIA, and in July of last year I celebrated my full reception into the Catholic Church. We had also been going to baptismal preparatory classes, and the children were baptized the same afternoon I entered the Church.

We have been blessed so much. Our parish is so full of beautiful, loving and giving people. We have made many friends, and they are very deep in their faith.

We have become very active in the Church. Our children love to go to Mass and CCD, and they make us very proud.

One thing which we are very excited about is our becoming a host couple for baptism preparation classes, which are held in different homes. We are really getting involved with it and our excitement overwhelms us sometimes. We've learned so much because of our journey, and we love to share it with others.

Our story began because of our quest for baptism. We are writing this to thank that Father who told us "no" in the beginning, because that actually led us to where we are right now. We've realized that this sacrament means dy-

ing and rising to new life with Christ, a life that depends
on faith, a community of believers, and a deep love for
God. And it happened to us.

Thank you to that priest for having the courage to
challenge us.   — *Maine*[1]

The following recommendations for the sacrament of baptism
flow from the ideas presented in the preceding chapters and correspond to the Church's official directives outlined in the last one.
They also represent procedures commonly practiced by those 100
or more clergy throughout the United States and Canada with
whom I discussed this issue of reaching out to marginal Catholics
in 1987-1988.

1. *Teach the ideal.*

The fundamental task of the clergy and of other pastoral leaders is one of teaching, not of enforcing. They are meant to serve as
inspiring religious instructors, not as monitoring police officers.

It is precisely here that the challenge, truth and consistency
aspects of this book find implementation.

The Church, as we have said, has always been able to sketch
in noble terms the ideal, while accommodating itself with patience
to the real. It constantly points out the call to holiness and the future everlasting destiny that are the twin vocations of every Christian. Yet, at the same time, it never stops proclaiming the limitless
mercy of God and the gentle forgiveness of the Spirit. It summons
us ever to be more, but understands where in our human weakness
we may be now.

Stressing the ideal, therefore, is an important part of ministering to those who seek baptism for their children.

This teaching responsibility means emphasizing how baptism
is a marvelous gift from God, necessary for salvation, bestowing
upon the infant divine grace through the faith of the Church and
the parents or their substitutes. It means explaining how the sacra-

ment presupposes and requires a well-founded hope that the newly baptized will be given a Christian formation until they reach maturity and reaffirm on their own the promises made years earlier by parents and godparents. It means explicating the practical ramifications of this training in the faith such as the good example of the parents, actual membership in the parish, regular involvement in the community's eucharistic worship and steady participation in religious education programs.

The rite itself teaches all these things in a powerful, even if generic way. For example, the direct questions at the beginning of the ritual, the promises before the actual pouring of water and pronouncement of formula, and the multiple blessing at the end speak to this responsibility for the religious education of the child. "They and their wives will be the first teachers of their child in the ways of the faith. May they also be the best of teachers, bearing witness to the faith by what they say and do...."[2]

The homily, which should be "short," is meant to explain the significance of the scriptural readings and also to lead those present "to a deeper understanding of the mystery of baptism and to encourage the parents and godparents to a ready acceptance of the responsibilities which arise from the sacrament" (no. 82).

While these few words of the homily should stress the parental duties to nurture the seed of baptismal grace about to be sown in the infant's heart, the preacher would be well advised to do so with gentleness. To use those moments instead for harsh condemnations of marginal Catholics and heavy-handed admonitions about fidelity to Mass will more likely infuriate participants than inspire them.

One young pastor in the Midwest finds that the baptismal preparation classes are the best occasions for spelling out parental responsibilities; he mentions those duties in the homily, but lightly and indirectly.

Pastoral people, reflecting upon past experiences with baptisms, may beat their breasts and wear worried expressions because many parents who passed through the preparation course still do not make it to Mass each Sunday. While that is regrettable, the more pertinent questions are: "Did we teach well? Did we clearly and with as much conviction as possible portray the Church's hope for the baptized? Did we sketch with realistic enthusiasm the Christian ideal?"

If they can give an affirmative answer to those questions, then these conscientious leaders should simply relax and leave the marginal ones in God's hands.

2. *Insist, but with flexibility, on parental participation in some sort of educational and formational preparation.*

While for reasons explained later we do not encourage the practice of making Mass attendance a requirement for baptism, we would support the policy of mandating some type of preparation program for the parents or their substitutes. One can find ample explicit support for such a general requirement in the official directives noted in the previous chapter. There needs to be a great flexibility in the application of this norm, however. A specific educational and formational preparation program set up for a particular parish is *not* the only way that such a responsibility can be fulfilled.

All institutions, including the Church, must fight a tendency to become fixed, rigid and unbending. While a well-planned, efficiently organized and expertly implemented parish baptismal program is praiseworthy and the procedure for most, there will always be a need to make exceptions for special circumstances.

> What if an unwed mother is too embarrassed to attend a session with other couples?
> What if a single parent works in the evening and cannot participate at the scheduled time?
> What if one parent cannot or will not come, as in the case of the letter introducing Chapter 4?
> What if the sponsors are out of town?

What if this is the second, third, fourth or more child and the parents have already been to a baptismal preparation class?

I have heard, unfortunately, too many "horror stories" of cases in which the parents were told either to comply with the scheduled parish baptismal course or to accept having their child denied the sacrament.

A single hour session on a one-to-one basis between the parent(s) and the clergy or pastoral minister should be sufficient to cover the needed topics in a situation requiring specialized attention. More extended, group programs may be desirable and helpful, but may we impose them as obligations required before any baptism?

Official directives suggest a very wise procedure: Before the child is born the parents, if possible, should inform the parish clergy of the approaching event and participate in the preparation course during the pregnancy and prior to the child's birth.[3]

Both parents frequently attend early on birthing classes to assist them with the pregnancy, delivery and early moments of the infant's life. In similar fashion, consistent instruction from the pulpit and in the bulletin encouraging expectant parents to participate in the baptismal course before the child is born may influence more and more of them to do so. Parents thus with fewer distractions and time pressures might derive greater benefit from the sessions in preparation for baptism.

Some creative parishes have developed enrichment baptismal classes for parents who are seeking the baptism of their second or third child and who already have attended the basic session when their first infant was baptized.

Needless to say, the classes should be attractively designed for effective adult education including good process, audio-visuals, printed take-home materials and engaging presentations.

3. *Involve lay persons in the formational sessions.*

The documents of the Second Vatican Council support this recommendation both indirectly by giving it a theological base and directly by explicitly calling for such a ministry.

The *Dogmatic Constitution on the Church* notes that as members of the People of God, each person through birth and baptism has a right and responsibility to build up God's kingdom.[4]

The *Decree on the Apostolate of Lay People* makes this theological teaching practically specific. Among the works of the family apostolate it lists "assisting engaged couples to make a better preparation for marriage," "taking a share in catechism-teaching," and "supporting married people and families in a material and moral crisis."[5]

That same document makes use of and endorses this phrase, the apostolate of "like towards like" (no. 13).

The *Rite of Christian Initiation* spells this out in connection with baptism. It says that "Christian instruction and the preparation for baptism are a vital concern of God's people, the Church, which hands on and nourishes the faith it has received from the apostles…. Therefore, it is most important that catechists and other lay people should work with priests and deacons in making preparations for baptism."[6]

Involvement of lay persons in baptismal preparation programs, therefore, has a solid theological base and the explicit endorsement of the Church. But it also responds to a practical necessity and adds great pastoral value to the sessions.

The declining number of clergy through deaths, resignations and a dearth of vocations makes the employment of lay persons as helpers in this educational and formational effort almost a necessity if we are to lift some of the burdens from the priest's or deacon's shoulders.

However, even more, the use of lay persons possesses a pastoral value which is hard to measure. This value is in the "like towards like" dimension of their efforts. When lay persons who are committed to Christ, loyal to the Church, active in the parish and dedicated, believing parents serve in the baptismal preparation ministry, their faith-filled lives make a great impact upon those seeking a child's baptism.

The clergy, in a sense or at least in the perception of lay persons, are supposed to be prayerful believers; it, moreover, is their "job" or profession to advise the parents about baptism and its obligations. But laity are volunteers doing these things simply because they believe in the sacraments and in the Church. This example and testimony about the importance of faith can powerfully influence the minds and hearts of those who seek baptism for their infants.

The baptismal program of a new parish in the Toronto suburbs illustrates such active participation of lay persons in the formation process.[7] Coordinated by one couple, the team has a total of ten couples. That parish averages 240 baptisms each year. The pastor first personally interviews the parents who seek their child's baptism and completes some initial data gathering.

The parents must then attend a session held each month on a Monday night from 7:30-9:00. One team couple conducts the session, but all ten are present. Each set of parents is assigned to a team couple. Within ten days that team couple visits the designated home, talks about baptism, explores the parents' faith practice and gathers the needed additional information. Attendance at the Monday meeting is a requirement. In five years they have postponed the baptism of but three infants.

The operative concept in that Canadian parish is twofold: First, you win more with a touch of honey than you do with a dose of vinegar. Second, through baptism a seed is planted, but unless there is an example of going to church regularly, the seed will not grow. About 60 to 70 percent of the parish participates faithfully in Sunday Mass.

4. Discuss arrangements during a personal visit, not over the telephone.

In Chapter 6 we described in some detail the high-risk elements involved with the first visit of a couple who seek marriage in the Church. At that time we also mentioned the dangers of discussing such arrangements over the telephone.

While the high-risk elements for various reasons normally are not as strong when parents ask for baptism, they still exist. Moreover, all the liabilities of telephone exchanges as opposed to personal interviews hold true for baptism as well as for matrimony.

At a large church in the Southeast I overheard the charming and efficient parish secretary make arrangements for baptism over the telephone with a parent who called. The staff person was cordial, gracious and positive. But the questions she posed, while legitimate enough, were potentially very explosive: Are you registered in this parish? Were you married by a priest? Do the godparents have a note indicating that they are good, practicing Catholics? In addition she explained the necessity of coming to the baptismal classes, an item which likewise can be a source of misunderstanding or conflict.

The secretary that day certainly possessed all the grace and tact one could hope for in any person responding to telephone inquiries. But how would she react on a "bad" day which every person occasionally suffers? Furthermore, what if those questions about such delicate matters as marital and religious status struck problem situations which the caller either admitted or concealed out of fear that the request would be rejected? Finally, is it not impossible for her over the telephone to gauge the person's response, positive or negative, to the requirement of attendance at a preparation session for baptism?

At a suburban parish in the Northeast, parents inquiring over the telephone about baptism are told they will be mailed a packet of information concerning the sacrament. This contains, in addition to educational literature, a form explaining their baptismal classes with a list of the time, dates and addresses of the homes in which they are held. After they complete one of the sessions, then the parents are to call the rectory for arrangement of the actual baptism.

There are many praiseworthy elements in the approach of that suburban church to the sacrament. But this impersonal, "over the telephone and through the mail" aspect leaves much to be desired.

At a parish in Kentucky that annually baptizes about 75 babies, the parents must sit down with the pastor for a visit before moving on to the baptismal classes offered twice each month. These exchanges enable him to get to know the parents, discuss their spiritual status, register them in the parish and encourage them to become more active members of the faith community.

Arranging baptisms through personal interviews will require considerable time and energy. But the certain good to be achieved and the possible harm to be avoided by following this practice warrants the expenditure of both.

5. *Have the presiding liturgist, priest or deacon meet with the parents before the actual celebration of baptism.*

We have spoken about the need and wisdom of engaging lay persons in the baptismal formation program. It would be regrettable, however, if this valuable development reduced the role of the priest or deacon simply to the liturgist who appears for the first time to the parents at the baptism. The idea of being a sacramental dispenser with little relationship to the worshiping community deeply troubles many of the clergy today, particularly those ordained in recent years. It also runs dangerously close to a magical or mechanical view of the sacraments.

Some contact, then, between presiding priest or deacon and the parents of the children to be baptized during the formation and preparation process is important. It could take place during the arrangement interview, in one of the formal classes or at the liturgical preparation session which we will describe below.

6. *Encourage parish registration, but do not mandate reception or use of church envelopes as a requisite for baptism.*

As proponents of sacrificial giving urge, there are many valuable benefits for parishioners, young or old, and for the parish to be gained from regular use of church envelopes.[8] But insisting on their use as a requisite for baptism is not justifiable.

First of all, by the very fact of residence within the territory of a certain parish, a person acquires a domicile there and the right to baptism in that church.[9]

Secondly, the Church allows baptism to take place in other churches with considerable latitude. "A just cause," "grave inconvenience," "a grave cause," "in case of necessity," or "some other compelling reason" are legal words covering the reasons needed for baptism outside of one's parish church.[10] To establish additional requirements, like envelope use, when canonical legislation offers this significant flexibility is at the very least inconsistent with the attitude of the universal Church.

Thirdly, in certain dioceses lay persons may join a parish outside their territorial boundaries and be entitled to all the sacraments from that church as long as they formally affiliate with it. This is normally accomplished by signing up to receive church envelopes. In such circumstances, the pastor or local clergy may insist on such registration and willingness to receive envelopes before the baptism of infants. Even in those situations, however, to require actual use of the envelopes before agreeing to baptize a child is questionable policy.

Once again, the issue is not the ideal or desirability of parish registration and use of church envelopes, but the requirement or necessity of both for baptism. We teach the ideal, but impose the minimal.

7. *Avoid making Mass attendance a requirement for baptism.*

This is perhaps the nub of the issue with regard to marginal Catholics and baptism.

At a large parish in the Southwest, one clergyman informed a young couple seeking baptism for their child that they should start going to Sunday Mass and after three weeks of seeing them at church, he would discuss the possibility of baptism. When they asked how he would know they were at the Eucharist in such a huge building, the clergyman told them to tug at his alb when he passed by them during the service.

We have already cited the case in Oklahoma of the priest who responded to a grandparent, "When the parents start going to Mass on Sundays, then we will talk about the baptism."

I have heard a pastor in the Northeast maintain with deep intensity that for parents to have their children baptized and not to come regularly to Sunday Eucharist is "unauthentic, a lie, unconscionable." Baptism, he stresses, is a welcoming into the Catholic Christian community; not to be a regular part of the central act of this community is thus inconsistent and not to be encouraged or tolerated.

The desire on the part of these persons to encourage commitment and fidelity among parishioners is noble indeed; to insist on regular Mass attendance as a condition for baptism is something entirely different.

The Church, of course, proclaims the great worth of the liturgy, especially the Eucharist. It is "the summit toward which the activity of the Church is directed; it is also the fount from which all her power flows.... From the liturgy, therefore, and especially from the Eucharist, grace is poured forth upon us as from a fountain...."[11] She, therefore, encourages and desires that every member have a great love for the Eucharist and obliges the faithful to participate in Mass every Sunday and holy day of obligation.[12]

But in the various official documents from which we excerpted sections in the previous chapter, one finds no mention of Mass attendance as a requisite for baptism. Clearly those decrees imply and infer that regular participation in the Eucharist is an integral part of Christian formation. But they do not mention that as an essential requirement for the baptismal sacrament. On the other hand, these decrees are very explicit about the educational and formational preparation progress needed before baptism.

We mentioned in Chapter 1 the danger of identifying faith with external faith practices. The Hispanic Catholic community in particular resents using Mass attendance as a barometer to measure the existence and degree of their faith. Moreover, many of them have emigrated from areas in which opportunities for the Eucharist each Sunday did not exist.

In Chapter 4 we cited Monsignor Philip Murnion's observations about our contemporary loss or lack of sacramental conviction of faith. One of the items he noted in support of his thesis was the use of baptismal and matrimonial strategies to bring about the socializing of Church members. The main purpose of such policies thus becomes an attempt to use these rites to cultivate more faithful Church practice (Sunday Mass). This differs greatly from the concept that people in practice need the grace of the sacraments.

In other words, baptism here becomes a club to compel Mass attendance. Celebration of the sacraments (in this case baptism) is a reward for being good and committed rather than a means to help us grow and become better persons. The long-standing tradition of the Church follows the latter emphasis, not the former one. Besides all these theoretical obstacles to insisting on Mass attendance as a requisite for baptism, there is this pragmatic one. Parents may well respond (sometimes with resentment) by participating in the Eucharist for a few weeks to satisfy the demands imposed. But when the celebration of baptism is over, they most likely will return to former patterns.

The familiar refrain occurs again: Preach, teach, explain, exhort, encourage the ideal of regular Sunday Mass participation; beware of making it a requirement for baptism.

8. *Treat each request for baptism on an individual basis according to the general principles which the Church has issued.*

Some years ago *Megatrends* captured the attention of Americans, staying on the *New York Times* bestseller list of books for 60 weeks.[13] In it author John Naisbitt described ten new directions in today's society which are transforming our lives. One is what he terms the development of a high tech/high touch society.

The high-tech trend represents, of course, the explosion of technological progress. Computers, cellular telephones, microsurgery and robots are examples of new inventions not even dreamed in the recent past.

But this upward growth has brought with it a downside regression — the dehumanization of our culture, the reduction of ourselves to numbers, the elimination or at least reduction of personal connections in our daily lives. Telephone and banking services are sample illustrations. Dial for information or phone repairs and you get unhelpful recordings; ask for simple adjustments in a fiscal transaction and you are told that the bank's computer cannot deal with such variations.

Those negative effects of high tech have led to what Naisbitt terms the high-touch movement in contemporary society. "Our response to the high tech all around us was the evolution of a highly personal value system to compensate for the impersonal nature of technology." We resent losing our human individuality, being reduced to a number and facing machines instead of people all day.

This reactionary high-touch development understandably has carried over into the life of the Church. The attitude of engaged couples during the last two decades is a case in point. Prior to the Second Vatican Council the nuptial liturgy was identical for every bride and groom. Since the early seventies, on the contrary, each couple has wanted and, with the help of the revised Catholic marriage rite, been able to fashion a wedding celebration which is distinctly their own, different from all others and personal to them.

The major emphasis of this high-touch personalism applies to our consideration of parents seeking the baptism of children. They are all different, come from diverse backgrounds and bring distinct circumstances to the baptismal arrangement meeting. Each father and mother wishes to be treated as a unique person and should be.

In small parishes with few baptisms, that personal, individualized approach probably happens almost naturally, especially if the clergy are sensitive, caring and flexible. But in larger churches with many baptisms, an impersonal, computerized-like style can emerge with unfortunate results simply because of the huge numbers involved. It will take keen awareness, hard work and considerable time for the clergy and pastoral leaders in such mammoth parishes to bring about a high-touch personal style into baptismal programs.

Treating each request for baptism on this individualized basis opens the possibility for the clear-sighted and understanding dialogue with the parents called for by the Vatican document on baptism. That facilitates from the very start the establishment of a cordial and caring relationship between the Church representative and the parents. It enables the clergy and parish ministers to discover the background of the parents, their current faith status and their attitudes toward baptism. It provides the opportunity then to design an educational/formational plan tailored to the particular religious needs of the parents. This is real, down-to-earth evangelization, taking the mother and father from where they are in their faith and seeking to lead them to a higher plateau.

The ultimate question in this individual dialogue for both parents and Church representative, however, remains, "Will he baptize our child?" or "Should the child be baptized?"

Countless clergy have asked for specific rules from their bishops to guide them in these sometimes perplexing situations. We actually already possess those norms, but they are general principles which consign the ultimate decision or judgment to the pastor. That leaves many priests and deacons feeling terribly burdened by such a responsibility and, in my judgment, they seek relief from those worries in their search for diocesan regulations which would decide or judge each case. This is simply a legal and pastoral impossibility.

Relief for them can come instead from an accurate knowledge of the general principles for baptism and a proper understanding of their role as pastor.

The general principles, cited in the previous chapter, are two-fold:

1. There must be a "founded hope" (*spes fundata*) that the baptism will bear fruit by the child being brought up in the Catholic religion.
2. Any pledge giving such a well-founded hope deserves to be considered as sufficient.[14]

The role of the pastor is to interpret those principles and apply them to the parents before him. He will need to preserve the quality of consistency and truth in this personalized dialogue by explaining the Church's hopes for the baptized and the parents, thereby challenging them to be more in the process. This is to "teach the ideal," the first recommendation made earlier. But the pastor also must observe the quality of compassion and mercy in this dialogue by the way he accepts at face value their promise, pledge or assurance that they will give the child a Christian formation.

Several Church axioms could be kept in mind as the pastor seeks to deal compassionately and in a kindly loving way with the parents, especially those who are marginal in their practice of the faith:

- The fact that the parents contact the parish and seek baptism creates a presumption about their good will and their desire to raise the child as Catholic.
- If in doubt, judge in favor of the person.
- The sacraments are for the good of the people. *Sacramenta sunt propter homines.*
- In Church laws, "favors are to be multiplied; burdens are to be restricted."
- The sacraments not only presuppose, but also strengthen and deepen faith.

In a word, the pastor is to judge or decide here and now whether the parents are promising, pledging or assuring him that they will raise the child Catholic. It is not his burden or responsibility to decide or judge whether they have or have not lived in the past or will or will not in the future live as active, practicing Catholics. If they have not, that is sad; if they do not in the future, that is too bad. His teaching efforts speak to those points. But in this function as decider or judge, he looks only at their present intention and presumes their sincerity. He is not the guarantor of conduct, the enforcer of rules or the monitor of behavior. That would be a worrisome task and a heavy burden indeed.

There is a parallel between this situation and that of an addictive penitent. The confessor presumes good will and accepts the stated purpose of amendment despite the bad past record and the unpromising future. Even with those who have slipped repeatedly, the recidivists, we continually offer them hope and forgiveness based on their present intentions.

A former theological seminary rector taught his students this governing sacramental norm which is more profound, solidly based and pastorally wise than it may sound: "If in doubt, give it out."

The practice of the Florida priest described in this book's Introduction serves, in my judgment, as a good model for pastors. He visits with the parents in their homes, explains the ritual of baptism and asks if they could say "yes" to the promises. When they answer affirmatively, he proceeds with the baptism.

The letter beginning this chapter featured a sharp challenge to a non-practicing interreligious couple who sought the baptism of their children. It caused anger and hurt, but had a happy ending. Challenging parents is necessary and can produce positive results.

But I wonder if the story of the Maine couple may be more of an exception than a rule. I fear that often what are intended as well-meaning challenges by the clergy become crushing experiences that break the bruised reed and snuff out the smouldering wick of faith within weak people. I think that compassion more than challenge is needed in today's Church, a compassionate acceptance of pledges now which may lead later to more active living out of faith.

9. *Delay, never refuse baptism.*

The Vatican directives are explicit about this. One should speak not of refusing baptism, but only delaying the sacrament until the family can grow in the faith or become more aware of the responsibilities connected with the baptism of their children.[15]

Even though these precise words are employed, the usually annoyed parents will probably still label the experience as a refusal of baptism.

If the concepts and suggestions of this book and chapter are observed, situations in which delays are in order should be rare. Priests of the Toronto parish described above delayed only three out of 720 in three years.

But should the lack of sufficient assurance about the infant's Christian upbringing dictate delay, the following pastoral approach used by a few clergy might prove valuable. The pastor concludes the session by saying, "You have indicated that you are not presently willing to give the Church a pledge or promise you will raise the child as a Catholic as we have discussed. The Church needs an assurance and assumes that a baptized infant will be given a Christian formation. Why don't you go home to pray and think about this matter. When you have decided to make such a pledge or assurance, contact us and we will be delighted to baptize your child."

10. *Involve parents in the liturgical celebration and support them after the baptism.*

Here are some practical suggestions for the active participation of the parents, godparents and others in the baptismal rite:

- When baptism takes place outside of Sunday Mass in therefore a somewhat smaller and less structured setting, participants could be invited to read the scriptures, responsorial psalm, petitions of the general intercessions and invocations of the saints. If the number to be baptized are few, this can be worked out informally that day; if the number are many, it may be necessary or certainly desirable to have a "rehearsal" for the parents beforehand to determine the readers and organize the rite.

- Baptism within Sunday Mass automatically involves the community and participants in a unique and praiseworthy way. There are some cautions to be noted, however. First, the rite mentions that baptism within Sunday Mass should "not be done too often."[16] Rotating baptism to different Masses so that it occurs about twice a year at a particular Eucharist seems a good pastoral procedure. Second, involvement of parents or godparents in liturgical ministries such as lectors or eucharistic ministers at Sunday Mass can be problematic in terms of suitable training, expertise and coordination with others regularly designated for those functions. Third, providing for baptism only at Sunday Mass seems unjustifiably restrictive, imposing needless burdens on those who for whatever reason prefer not to have their children baptized within the weekend Eucharist.

- A plain candle distributed as a gift beforehand accompanied by instructions on how to decorate it with suitable symbols can please parents and tap their creativity. Otherwise, commercial versions, already decorated and boxed with a flier containing a ceremony for the anniversary renewal of baptismal promises, serves the purpose well.

- A quantity of invitational fliers with spaces indicating the name, date and place of the forthcoming baptism can be given to the parents at the preparation class. They in turn complete them and mail the invitations to relatives and friends.

- A small choir might volunteer to assist with the celebration of baptism when done outside of Sunday Mass.

Here are several recommendations for providing support to the parents after the baptism:

- List the names of infants baptized and their parents in the parish bulletin.

- Bless the children when they come up to communion in the arms or by the side of parents.

- Acknowledge as presiding priest the presence of children during the Mass.

- Send out at regular intervals informational or inspirational fliers to the parents.

- Plan special liturgies for children following the ideas contained in the *Directory for Children's Liturgies*.

Conclusion

In our previous discussions we have mentioned how current studies indicate that great numbers of Catholic young people distance themselves from the Church during late adolescence and do not return until their late twenties. This means that many of those who seek baptism for their children are still in those unsettled, questioning years. Admonishing them too severely about their religious marginalism and insisting too strongly on conversion to active Catholicism at that time often meets with open or submerged hostility to institutional religion and worship. More effective could be the gentle and compassionate approach which seeks to keep alive this weak flame of faith with the hope that it will eventually burst into a roaring, fervent fire. This change or conversion is more likely to occur chronologically at the First Communion of the oldest child than at the parent's marriage or at the baptism of the initial infant.

An awareness of this development should lead those in the baptismal ministry to carry out their tasks with compassion, patience and hope, conscious that the good they are doing now may not bear fruit until several years later.

Guidance from the *Catechism*

Article 1250: "Born with a fallen human nature and tainted by original sin, children also have need of the new birth in Baptism to be freed from the power of darkness and brought into the realm of the freedom of the children of God, to which all men are called (cf. Council of Trent (1546): DS 1514; cf. *Col* 1:12-24). The sheer gratuitousness of the grace of salvation is particularly manifest in infant Baptism. The Church and the parents would deny a child the priceless grace of becoming a child of God were they not to confer Baptism shortly after birth" (cf. CIC, can. 867; CCEO, can. 681; 686, 1).

Article 1253: "Baptism is the sacrament of faith (cf. *Mk* 16:16). But faith needs the community of believers. It is only within the faith of the Church that each of the faithful can believe. The faith required for Baptism is not a perfect and mature faith, but a beginning that is called to develop."

Article 1254: "For all the baptized, children or adults, faith must grow *after* Baptism. For this reason the Church celebrates each year at the Easter Vigil the renewal of baptismal promises. Preparation for Baptism leads only to the threshold of new life. Baptism is the source of that new life in Christ from which the entire Christian life springs forth."

Article 1255: "For the grace of Baptism to unfold, the parents' help is important. So too is the role of the *godfather* and *godmother*, who must be firm believers, able and ready to help the newly baptized—child or adult—on the road of Christian life (cf. CIC, can. 872-874). Their task is a truly ecclesial function (*officium*) (cf. *SC* 67). The whole ecclesial community bears some responsibility for the development and safeguarding of the grace given at Baptism."

9

Marriage: Official Directives

I am a very religious Catholic woman who tried to give the best example to my children. Both attended Catholic schools.

My daughter, who was a teacher in a Catholic high school and went to church regularly, was going to be married in our parish. Her fiancé, raised in a Catholic family and Catholic schools, had abandoned the Church.

I went to our parish to make the arrangements for the wedding. One of the priests, who was a very devout clergyman and had known my daughter for years, questioned me about the groom. I answered truthfully.

His tone of voice changed and abruptly he said, "Oh! Dear Lord, a renegade! I hope you are not coming to ask me to perform the ceremony, because I would not touch that man with a ten foot pole."

I was really shocked and those words stayed in my mind to this day. I never intended to ask him to perform the ceremony. I had another priest in mind whom I greatly admired.

My daughter never knew about this encounter. I was so afraid it would change her attitude toward the Church. The other priest I talked to told me it would be an honor to perform the ceremony. But I was so scared about his reaction that I hid the fact that my future son-in-law was a marginal Catholic.

My daughter has been married 12 years. Her husband is a devoted father. He still doesn't practice, but never misses the special children's Masses and volunteers often for church events. My daughter prays that God will send him the necessary graces to become a good Catholic.

Recently my mood was uplifted! I was invited to a christening and was wondering how that baby was going to be baptized in Church knowing that the parents are not only marginal Catholics but were married by a minister (they had a difference of opinion with the parish priest).

After their wedding they had moved to another part of the city. I expressed my surprise to the young couple. They had explained the situation to the priest. He was very warm and understanding. They were very much impressed by him and told me it was an incentive for them to go back to Church.

The ceremony was beautiful. The celebrant touched everyone's heart, explaining the duties of parents and god-parents at length. Even the most indifferent Catholic in our group left with a better understanding of the sacrament and praise for the priest.

I think demanding Church attendance as a condition for baptism or matrimony is wrong. It alienates young people even more. I have seen examples of people turning to another faith. More leniency would bring them closer to the Church. God in his infinite wisdom maybe would choose that special moment to touch their hearts.

I am glad I have the opportunity to write (very poorly) on the subject. Excuse my English which is not my language.   — New York

This chapter, like Chapter 7 on the official directives related to baptism, will be rather dry and technical. It also presents the authentic teaching of the Catholic Church, this time on matrimony, through three Vatican documents: the Rite of Marriage published in 1969; *The Christian Family in the Modern World* (*Familiaris Consortio*), an Apostolic Exhortation issued by Pope John Paul II on December 15, 1981; and the 1983 *Code of Canon Law.*

As in the case of baptism, these offer general guidelines and even some specific norms, but they, too, leave ultimate decisions about a particular marriage to the local clergy.

Rite of Marriage

The Introduction of this ritual is considerably shorter than the comparable one for baptism. As a consequence it provides only slight and indirect guidance for the clergy and pastoral ministers in dealing with marginally Catholic engaged couples who seek marriage in the Church.

The first four paragraphs of a section on the "Importance and Dignity of the Sacrament of Matrimony" explicitly cover those two topics of the title. In the typically succinct, doctrinally rich style of ritual introductions, they treat concepts such as the sublime purpose of marriage, irrevocable consent, unbreakable union and total fidelity between husband and wife essential for this state, its dual purpose of mutual love and the procreation/education of children, the mystery of matrimony and its elevation by Christ to the level of a sacrament (nos. 1-4).

The Introduction does provide the clergy with an overall theme or thrust for their marriage preparation efforts. "Priests should first of all strengthen and nourish the faith of those about to be married, for the sacrament of matrimony presupposes and demands faith" (no. 7).

Two paragraphs suggest practical ways to achieve this strengthening and nourishing of the bridal pair's faith: the preparatory instructions and the liturgical celebration itself.

A priest should bear in mind these principles of faith, both in his instructions to those about to be married and when giving the homily during the marriage ceremony. He should relate his instructions to the texts of the sacred readings.

The bridal couple should be given a review of the fundamentals of Christian doctrine. This may include instruction on the teachings about marriage and the family, on the rites used in the celebration of the sacrament itself, and on the prayers and readings. In this way the bridegroom and the bride will receive far greater benefit from the celebration.

In the celebration of marriage (which normally should be within the Mass), certain elements should be stressed, especially the liturgy of the word, which shows the importance of Christian marriage in the history of salvation and the duties and responsibility of the couple in caring for the holiness of their children. Also of supreme importance are the consent of the contracting parties, which the priest asks and receives; the special nuptial blessing for the bride and for the marriage covenant; and finally, the reception of Holy Communion by the groom and the bride, and by all present, by which their love is nourished and all are lifted up into communion with our Lord and with one another (nos. 5-6).

In a surprisingly sensitive and pastorally astute recommendation, the ritual urges the clergy to display a special concern for those at the liturgical celebration who are not Catholic or who rarely come to Mass or who seemed to have abandoned the faith.

Furthermore, priests should show special consideration to those who take part in liturgical celebrations or hear the gospel only on the occasion of a wedding, either because they are not Catholics, or because they are Catholics who rarely, if ever, take part in the Eucharist or seem to have abandoned the practice of their faith. Priests are ministers of Christ's gospel to everyone (no. 9).

In a section giving rubrical details, the ritual comments that "the liturgy of the word is extremely helpful in emphasizing the meaning of the sacrament and the obligations of marriage" (no. 11).

The Christian Family in the Modern World

This apostolic exhortation issued by Pope John Paul II in 1981 provides the most useful guidance in our discussion of reaching out to marginal Catholics. The entire document deserves a close reading. Here we cite only excerpts from two sections, one on marriage preparation and the other on the celebration of marriage and the evangelization of non-believing baptized persons.

The Holy Father notes the unique importance and necessity in our day of preparation for marriage and family life.

> More than ever necessary in our times is preparation of young people for marriage and family life. In some countries it is still the families themselves that, according to ancient customs, ensure the passing on to young people of the values concerning married and family life, and they do this through a gradual process of education or initiation. But the changes that have taken place within almost all modern societies demand that not only the family but also society and the Church should be involved in the effort of properly preparing young people for their future responsibilities.
>
> Many negative phenomena which are today noted with regret in family life derive from the fact that in the new situations young people not only lose sight of the correct hierarchy of values but, since they no longer have certain criteria of behavior, they do not know how to face and deal with the new difficulties. But experience teaches that young people who have been well prepared for family life generally succeed better than others.
>
> This is even more applicable to Christian marriage,

which influences the holiness of large numbers of men and
women. The Church must therefore promote better and
more intensive programs of marriage preparation in order
to eliminate as far as possible the difficulties that many
married couples find themselves in, and even more in order to favor positively the establishing and maturing of
successful marriages (no. 66).

We normally throughout this country think of marriage
preparation in terms of the programs and activities immediately
prior to the wedding celebration. They would include visits with
the clergy, some type of educational/formational course, class or
experience, planning of the liturgy and the rehearsal. Pope John Paul
II expands our vision, however, and views marriage preparation as
a "gradual and continuous process" embracing three main stages:

> *Remote preparation* begins in early childhood in that wise
> family training which leads children to discover themselves
> as beings endowed with a rich and complex psychology and
> with a particular personality with its own strengths and
> weaknesses. It is the period when esteem for all authentic
> human values is instilled, both in interpersonal and in
> social relationships, with all that this signifies for the for-
> mation of character, for the control and right use of one's
> inclinations, for the manner of regarding and meeting
> people of the opposite sex, and so on. Also necessary, es-
> pecially for Christians, is solid spiritual and catechetical
> formation that will show that marriage is a true vocation
> and mission, without excluding the possibility of the to-
> tal gift of self to God in the vocation to the priestly or re-
> ligious life.
>   Upon this basis there will subsequently and gradually
> be built up the *proximate preparation*, which — from the
> suitable age and with adequate catechesis, as in a
> catechumenal process — involves a more specific prepara-
> tion for the sacraments, as it were, a rediscovery of them.
> This renewed catechesis of young people and others pre-

paring for Christian marriage is absolutely necessary in order that the sacrament may be celebrated and lived with the right moral and spiritual dispositions. The religious formation of young people should be integrated, at the right moment and in accordance with the various concrete requirements, with a preparation for life as a couple. This preparation will present marriage as an interpersonal relationship of a man and woman that has to be continually developed, and it will encourage those concerned to study the nature of conjugal sexuality and responsible parenthood, with the essential medical and biological knowledge connected with it. It will also acquaint those concerned with correct methods for the education of children and will assist them in gaining the basic requisites for well-ordered family life, such as stable work, sufficient financial resources, sensible administration, notions of housekeeping.

Finally one must not overlook preparation for the family apostolate, for fraternal solidarity and collaboration with other families, for active membership in groups, associations, movements and undertakings set up for the human and Christian benefit of the family.

The *immediate preparation* for the celebration of the sacrament of matrimony should take place in the months and weeks immediately preceding the wedding so as to give a new meaning, content and form to the so-called premarital inquiry required by canon law. This preparation is not only necessary in every case, but is also more urgently needed for engaged couples that still manifest shortcomings or difficulties in Christian doctrine and practice.

Among the elements to be instilled in this journey of faith, which is similar to the catechumenate, there must also be a deeper knowledge of the mystery of Christ and the Church, of the meaning of grace and of the responsibility of Christian marriage, as well as preparation for taking an active and conscious part in the rites of the marriage liturgy.

The Christian family and the whole of the ecclesial

community should feel involved in the different phases of
the preparation for marriage which have been described
only in their broad outlines. It is to be hoped that the episcopal conferences, just as they are concerned with appropriate initiatives to help engaged couples to be more aware
of the seriousness of their choice and also to help pastors
of souls to make sure of the couples' proper dispositions,
so they will also take steps to see that there is issued a directory for the pastoral care of the family. In this they
should lay down in the first place, the minimum content,
duration and method of the "preparation courses," balancing the different aspects — doctrinal, pedagogical, legal
and medical — concerning marriage and structuring them
in such a way that those preparing for marriage will not
only receive an intellectual training, but will also feel a
desire to enter actively into the ecclesial community (no.
66).

Of a very particular interest to us are the pope's detailed,
tightly reasoned norms or guidelines for responding to couples who
seek marriage in the Church, but whose level of faith is minimal or
whose practice of the faith is quite irregular or almost non-existent
(no. 68).

For the sake of clarity and ease in reading we have slightly
rearranged the material of this section and made minor editing
changes in the text to fit that rearrangement. In dealing with an
engaged pair who wish to marry in the Church, but whose faith and
religious practice are questionable, Pope John Paul II provided these
principles which ran counter at that time to the current pastoral
practice in some areas of our country:

- The faith of the person(s) seeking marriage in the church can
  exist in varying degrees. It is the primary duty of pastors to
  facilitate a rediscovery, nourishing and maturing of this faith.
- The Church, however, also admits to the celebration of marriage those who are imperfectly disposed.
- A couple who decide to marry according to the divine plan,

that is, to commit their whole lives in unbreakable love and unconditional faithfulness by an irrevocable nuptial consent, are reflecting, even if not in a fully conscious way, an attitude of profound obedience to God's will, an attitude which cannot exist without God's grace.

- With such a decision or consent, the couple have entered upon a journey toward salvation, a journey which with their upright intention and through the immediate preparation and celebration of the sacrament can be complemented and brought to completion.

- The fact that couples often request marriage in the Church for social rather than genuinely religious reasons is understandable. However, the fact that motives of a social nature are present is not enough to justify refusal by the pastor to celebrate the marriage.

- Engaged couples, by baptism, already really share in Christ's marriage covenant with the Church. Moreover, by their right intention, described above, they have accepted God's plan for marriage. Therefore, given these two points, they at least implicitly consent to what the Church intends to do when she celebrates marriage.

- Insisting on further criteria that concern the faith level of the couple as a requirement for admission to the Church celebration of marriage involves great risks. It leads to the danger of making unfounded and discriminatory judgments, as well as to the peril of causing doubts about the validity of marriages already celebrated.

- Nevertheless, when engaged couples explicitly and formally reject what the Church intends to do in the marriage of baptized persons, the pastor cannot admit them to the celebration of the sacrament.

- The pastor in such circumstances must indicate to the couple his reluctance to defer the marriage and to stress that they, not the Church, are placing the obstacles to such a celebration.

The pope concludes this section with a reminder of the need

for "evangelization and catechesis before and after marriage, effected
by the whole Christian community, so that every man and woman
who gets married celebrates the sacrament of matrimony not only
validly but also fruitfully" (no. 68).

Code of Canon Law

The 1983 *Code of Canon Law* treats of marriage mainly, as in
the case of baptism, in Book IV, "The Office of Sanctifying in the
Church." Title VII covers this sacrament with canons 1055-1165,
a more extensive section containing 110 canons as opposed to the
39 in the corresponding part for baptism. There are ten chapters
in Title VII, but most of them deal with technical matters such as
diriment impediments, matrimonial consent, mixed and secret
marriages, separation of spouses and convalidation of marriages.
While these naturally relate to the issue of marginal Catholics and
marriage in the Church, the canons more pertinent to our precise
concerns are found in the introduction and in chapter 1 on "Pastoral Care and What Must Precede Celebration of Marriage."

The following canons spell out the nature of any Christian
marriage and matrimonial consent:

> The matrimonial covenant, by which a man and a woman
> establish between themselves a partnership of the whole of
> life, is by its nature ordered toward the good of the spouses
> and the procreation and education of offspring; this cov-
> enant between baptized persons has been raised by Christ
> the Lord to the dignity of a sacrament (canon 1055:1).
>
> The essential properties of marriage are unity and in-
> dissolubility, which in Christian marriage obtain a special
> firmness in virtue of the sacrament (canon 1056).
>
> Marriage is brought about through the consent of the
> parties, legitimately manifested between persons who are
> capable according to law of giving consent; no human
> power can replace this consent.

Matrimonial consent is an act of the will by which a man and woman through an irrevocable covenant, mutually give and accept each other in order to establish marriage (canon 1057:1, 2).

The Church jealously protects the couple's natural right to marriage, even though that right is not absolute and is circumscribed by the rights of others, including the secular society and the Church community. Three terse canons reflect that jealous concern.

All persons who are not prohibited by law can contract marriage (canon 1058).

Before marriage is celebrated, it must be evident that nothing stands in the way of its valid and licit celebration (canon 1066).

Marriage enjoys the favor of the law; consequently, when a doubt exists the validity of a marriage is to be upheld until the contrary is proven (canon 1060).

One lengthy canon outlines the ingredients of good pastoral care before and after marriage:

Pastors of souls are obliged to see to it that their own ecclesial community furnishes the Christian faithful assistance so that the matrimonial state is maintained in a Christian spirit and makes progress toward perfection. This assistance is especially to be furnished through:

1. Preaching, catechesis adapted to minors, youths and adults, and even the use of the media of social communications so that through these means the Christian faithful may be instructed concerning the meaning of Christian marriage and the duty of Christian spouses and parents;

2. Personal preparation for entering marriage so that through such preparation the parties may be predisposed toward the holiness and duties of their new state;

3. A fruitful liturgical celebration of marriage clarifying that the spouses signify and share in that mystery of unity and of fruitful love that exists between Christ and the Church;

4. Assistance furnished to those already married so that, while faithfully maintaining and protecting the conjugal covenant, they may day by day come to lead holier and fuller lives in their families (canon 1063).

Another canon proposes a sacramental ideal, the reception of confirmation, penance and Eucharist before matrimony.

If they can do so without serious inconvenience, Catholics who have not yet received the sacrament of confirmation are to receive it before being admitted to marriage.

It is strongly recommended that those to be married approach the sacraments of penance and the Most Holy Eucharist so that they may fruitfully receive the sacrament of marriage (canon 1065:1, 2).

The Code, of course, does mention the issue of questionable cases for marriage (e.g. canon 1071 for several dubious situations and canon 1072 for youths). It also outlines elements which render certain couples or individuals incapable of contracting marriage:

They are incapable of contracting marriage:

1. Who lack sufficient use of reason;

2. Who suffer from grave lack of discretion of judgment concerning essential matrimonial rights and duties which are to be mutually given and accepted;

3. Who are not capable of assuming the essential obligations of matrimony due to causes of a psychic nature (canon 1095:1-3).

Nevertheless, that primary natural right to marriage emerges again and, even in difficult cases, limits the local bishop's authority to delay or prohibit a marriage.

> In a particular case the local Ordinary can prohibit the marriage of his own subjects wherever they are staying and of all persons actually present in his own territory, but only for a time, for a serious cause and as long as that cause exists.
>
> Only the supreme authority of the Church can add an invalidating clause to a prohibition (canon 1077:1-2).

In our concluding chapter we will link together the data presented in this chapter and in chapters 1-6 by offering several practical, pragmatic or pastoral suggestions for responding to couples who seek marriage in the Church but who by our definition are marginal Catholics.

Guidance from the *Catechism*

Article 1601: "The matrimonial covenant, by which a man and a woman establish between themselves a partnership of the whole of life, is by its nature ordered toward the good of the spouses and the procreation and education of offspring; this covenant between baptized persons has been raised by Christ the Lord to the dignity of a sacrament" (CIC, can. 1055 §1; cf. GS 48 §1).

Article 1614: "In his preaching Jesus unequivocally taught the original meaning of the union of man and woman as the Creator willed it from the beginning: permission given by Moses to divorce one's wife was a concession to the hardness of hearts (cf. *Mt* 19:8). The matrimonial union of man and woman is indissoluble: God himself has determined it: 'what therefore God has joined together, let no man put asunder'" (*Mt* 19:6).

Article 1623: According to the Latin tradition, the spouses as ministers of Christ's grace mutually confer upon each other the sacrament of Matrimony by expressing their consent before the Church. In the traditions of the Eastern Churches, the priests (bishops or presbyters) are witnesses to the mutual consent given by the spouses (cf. CCEO, can. 817), but for the validity of the sacrament their blessing is also necessary (cf. CCEO, can. 828).

Article 1624: "The various liturgies abound in prayers of blessing and epiclesis asking God's grace and blessing on the new couple, especially the bride. In the epiclesis of this sacrament the spouses receive the Holy Spirit as the communion of love of Christ and the Church (cf. *Eph* 5:32). The Holy Spirit is the seal of their covenant, the ever-available source of their love and the strength to renew their fidelity."

10 Marriage: Pastoral Suggestions

I am at this stage of my life (35 years old, married, two children, working four days a week) fairly involved in a range of activities at my church. One year ago I was commissioned as a eucharistic minister. I recently celebrated my first independent communion service at one of our homes for the aged. I have been a "group captain" of our parish prayer line for the last five years. My major involvement with the Church is through my position as Spiritual Convener for the Catholic Women's League. I am responsible for arranging the liturgy for our monthly Mass, for organizing receptions for all new celebrants of the sacraments, and for doing whatever I can to encourage the faith of our members.

By now, I am sure that you are wondering why I am detailing all of these activities. I wanted to show you the degree of my involvement with the Church which I abandoned when I left home at 18. My father is a very devout man and when I left home, it was because of what were then irreconcilable differences between myself and my parents. My ceasing to attend church was just one of the ways I expressed my new independence.

I was, however, married in the Church and had both of my children promptly baptized because I could not conceive of any other option — it was the way to do these things. For ten years or so I attended church on occasion, but refrained from receiving communion as I knew very strongly how hypocritical it would have been.

Then, six years ago, my oldest child made her First Communion. I started bringing her to weekly Mass, as it was expected of the children, and mostly because their teacher asked them each Monday morning who went to Mass! Although our wedding and the baptisms were performed with no problem by the pastor who knew my in-laws very well, I was afraid that Margaret would not be allowed to make her First Communion with our new pastor unless we showed some sign of involvement with the Church. I also spent a lot of time helping to prepare her for this sacrament with a book sent home by the school each weekend.

When Margaret made her First Communion I felt that I had come home. And as my involvement with the Church grows, so do my blessings! The last few years have seen some truly miraculous, joyous occasions in my life, as well as the development of a better relationship with my husband and a dramatic improvement in our family finances. And yes, I do attribute all this to the Lord. And to the graces which flowed six years ago — not only to the little girl making her First Communion, but to me, her mother.

I beg you to continue to spread your view of challenging — not crushing — those who have wandered from the faith. Somewhere they hold a seedling, a remnant of what their faith once meant to them, and, as I am proof, the occasion of celebrating a family sacrament *can* provide the impetus to rediscover that faith and live it in exciting and meaningful ways which they never would have dreamt of at an earlier age.　　　　　　　　　　— *Canada*

Some of the practical recommendations for the sacrament of matrimony which follow are similar to those offered in Chapter 8 for baptism and some are totally different. But all of them do, like their counterparts for baptism, flow from the ideas presented in Chapters 1-6 and correspond to the Church's official directives outlined in the last chapter. They also reflect policies and procedures commonly practiced by the clergy with whom I dialogued about this issue of reaching out to marginal Catholics.[1]

1. *Make arrangements during a personal visit, never over the telephone.*

We analyzed at some length in Chapter 6 the many specific anxieties which engaged couples frequently carry with them when they begin their definitive preparations for marriage. Telephoning the church office or stopping to visit with the clergy after Sunday Mass is normally the first step in that process.

Such contact is what we term a "crisis" or turning point moment for them and one normally filled with a considerable degree of both excited hopes and nervous anticipation. As we mentioned in Chapter 6, if there are any complications at all in their personal situations, the nervousness and apprehension intensifies.

We have noted on several previous occasions the dangers which accompany handling those high-risk, potentially explosive first exchanges over the telephone. What is needed at these moments is simply a cordial tone of voice, several joyful words about love and marriage, an expressed willingness to help the couple and the establishment of an appointment within the near future to discuss details.

The mere reservation of a definite day and time for the formal meeting with the parish clergy will in almost all cases relieve the couple of their tension at this crisis moment. It means the process or journey to the altar has begun. They are now underway. The initial connection with the Church has been pleasant and positive. We have thus quite easily created a climate or set an atmosphere for all the sessions which will occur in the months ahead.

When the actual appointment arrives, the couple's anxieties will probably surface again. But their uneasiness will be greatly lessened because of that first brief, but encouraging encounter they had over the telephone or in person with the parish clergy.

2. If possible, have the priest or deacon who will preside at the liturgy conduct the initial interview.

In today's wedding liturgy, the presiding priest or deacon has a particularly important role to play. Since couples have the opportunity to select the readings, prayers and blessing they like as well as to incorporate certain creative elements of their own into the nuptial celebration, someone needs to blend together these many disparate ingredients. The presiding clergyman is the person who mainly fulfills that function. Because the bride and groom want their ceremony to move along smoothly and come off well, they recognize early on, therefore, that the priest or deacon who will lead the liturgy is crucial for its success.

First impressions are critical. They are even more so when initial encounters possess the kind of underlying intense dynamics we have described above.

Link those two items together — the importance of the presiding liturgist to the couple for the nuptial celebration's success and the power of initial impressions — and we have a justification for this second recommendation.

Other people will eventually become involved in the marital preparation process. Nevertheless, when the liturgical presider handles the initial interview well, he creates a close and respectful bond between himself and the couple which will prove highly beneficial later at the wedding rehearsal and nuptial service. They have come to know, like and trust him.

3. Extend a warm welcome.

Since couples seeking to arrange for marriage in the Church bring with them a high level of anxiety, it is important that the initial moments of the first personal interview establish a comfortable rapport and trusting atmosphere. One of the ways of doing this is to use a series of non-threatening questions at the start. I have employed the following set of inquiries for that purpose with perhaps 1,000 couples over the past decades.

• "Where do you work?"

The couple usually feel at ease and are obviously comfortable in conversing about the place and type of their employment. Doing so can also prove interesting as well as informative for the interviewing clergyman. It likewise serves as an icebreaker in speaking with the engaged pair.

Later, after the couple departs, it is good to make a few notes about this particular part of the discussion and insert them into the bride and groom's file. The data will seem fresh and indelible immediately following the interview, but those details will slip from memory in time and need refreshment before the next appointment.

A variation on this question is: "What is your trade or work?"

Another similar or additional start-up inquiry is: "Where did you come from?"

• "How did you meet?"

This question leads the couple almost imperceptibly toward areas that are more personal and intimate. Some humor on the part of the priest or deacon about this topic can help them relax and be honest. More of these love matches begin at local bars than at church picnics and it is helpful to acknowledge that reality in a light-hearted way.

• "What was your first impression of him?... of her?"

The exchange, while continuing on a rather surface and non-threatening plane, now dips deeper and can become more revealing. This may be the first time the couple have disclosed those long past immediate reactions to one another. The responses will vary greatly, with their comments often routine, but occasionally touching or laughable.

• "Why do you think you fell in love with each other?"

The interview now plunges rather quickly and profoundly into the nature of the couple's relationship. This question will generally leave the pair puzzled and unable to answer.

A few reflective thoughts from the priest or deacon about the falling in love experience can stimulate the discussion.

These might include, for example, the thinking of certain

contemporary psychologists that in our complex society the reasons why we fall in love with this particular person are so complicated and hidden that only in-depth analysis would reveal the hidden motives behind the phenomenon. Even the results of such a professional examination would still be highly conjectural.

These reflections could also cite the theory of other scholars that we have a tendency to fall in love with our ego complement, an individual who helps complete us, who helps fill up what is lacking in ourselves.

I have found that spending a few minutes stating these concepts and offering a few illustrations of them will frequently bring a nod of their heads or a knowing look between the engaged pair. The hypothetical cases could be a hot-tempered person matching with an even mannered individual, an always late with an always early partner, an extrovert with an introvert.

The purpose of this question and the exchange it prompts is not to develop an amateur analysis of their relationship, but merely to draw them into a potentially profound discussion about relationships in general and their own in particular.

• "What is his most endearing quality for you, right now? Hers?"

The couple may grow slightly embarrassed by this question, but they eventually will name one or a few characteristics. That exchange is affirming in itself, but also suggests a pattern of affirmation for the future.

These questions and the discussions which they prompt may consume five to twenty minutes depending upon the rapport between the clergy and the couple and upon the ability or willingness of the engaged pair to articulate their thoughts and feelings.

The hope, of course, is that those moments will create a cordial climate, manifest the clergy's loving concern for the couple and reduce the engaged pair's anxiety. Before any conversation about delicate or thorny issues like an interreligious marriage, annulments or inactive church attendance, these questions usually will have forged a good relationship between the priest or deacon and the couple. Then, if some difficult remarks must be made or hard choices proposed, the couple may be more disposed to hear those words and more inclined to make those choices.

4. *Use marital instruments or inventories as tools to promote dialogue, not as tests to measure the couple's readiness for marriage.*

A majority of dioceses in the United States use some type of premarital instrument or inventory to help foster discussion between the engaged couple.

The three most commonly employed in this country today have been:

FOCCUS (Facilitating Open Couple Communication, Understanding and Study) developed in 1984 by the Archdiocese of Omaha. Contact: FOCCUS, Family Life Office, 3214 N. 60th Street, Omaha, NE 68104.

PMI (Pre-Marital Inventory) developed by Bess Associates in 1975 and revised as PMI *Profile* from Intercommunication Publishing, Inc., in 1984. Contact: PMI *Profile*, Intercommunication Publishing, Inc., 1 Valentine Lane, Chapel Hill, NC 27514.

PREPARE-ENRICH, Inc. (Premarital Personal and Relationship Enrichment) was developed in 1977 by Dr. David H. Olson and his colleagues. Contact: Prepare-Enrich, Inc., P.O. Box 190, Minneapolis, MN 55440.

These instruments or inventories have proven to be extremely useful in promoting dialogue between the couple themselves and also between the couple and those involved in marriage preparation, including the clergy.

However, they should not be employed as a pass/fail test, a fixed diagnostic criterion of a couple's potential for a good marriage or as a single measure of whether or not a couple may be married in the Church. They are not intended to predict the future, but have been conceived simply to facilitate a process and to assist a couple in examining, understanding and communicating.

Nevertheless, there is a risk that those in marriage preparation will use them as tests or at least that they will be perceived by the engaged couple as tests which must be passed before they can marry in the Church.

5. *Insist, but in a flexible and open manner, upon some form of marriage preparation program.*

It is precisely in such a preparation program that pastoral ministers, including the clergy, can fulfill the principle of challenge, truth and consistency we have discussed in this book. It is here that we teach the ideal. It is during these sessions, for example, that we underscore the faith dimension of matrimony and the importance of support for the couple from the believing community assembled for the Eucharist on Sunday. It is at those meetings that the clergy and others sketch the dignity of the sacrament and the spiritual responsibilities which flow from it.

In the United States, over 90 percent of Roman Catholic dioceses offer marriage preparation programs and about 60 percent not only provide, but require participation in them. Pope John Paul II has observed, "Experience teaches that young people who have been well prepared for family life generally succeed better than others."[2]

It would be helpful in support of a policy mandating these sessions as a requisite for marriage if we had hard statistics which demonstrated that marital preparation programs reduce the incidence of divorce or separation among couples who participate in them.

Unfortunately, research scholars in our nation have concluded that for various reasons no empirical data exist to support this notion. We have, moreover, no statistical evidence that couples who participate in these preparatory sessions are more satisfied or successful in their marriages than those who do not. Finally, we possess no serious research which can determine whether marital preparation programs prevent bad marriages or not.

Still, a Canadian project has assembled some data that suggest couples are more likely to resolve conflicts and take other positive and preventive actions as a result of marital preparation sessions. Couples, according to this research, are more successful if they complete the program under study.

Despite limitations, therefore, we do have statistical studies which indicate that marriage preparation programs have been well received by engaged couples and appear to exert a positive influence upon them.

All of the above points lend support to the reasonableness of a parish policy or pastoral approach which requires some type of preparation program prior to celebration of marriage in the Church.

As with the case of baptism, however, there must be an open and flexible application of that regulation to each couple's circumstances. There are a variety of excellent programs in existence today, including creative arrangements on the parish level. Yet, to insist that the engaged pair participate in any one particular form, for example, Engaged Encounter, would be to take the reasonable general norm and unreasonably restrict it. In our highly mobile society, moreover, the prospective bride and groom are often separated during courtship. To demand, as another illustration, that they must attend the sessions together is likewise to impose an intolerable and unwarranted burden upon them.

Unless the local faith community has developed a corps of lay persons who can conduct one-to-one marriage preparation programs to cover those exceptional circumstances in which it is physically or otherwise impossible for the engaged pair to participate in some large group event, it would also seem unreasonable to maintain a mandatory policy in that parish. There must be a viable alternative for those who do not or cannot fit into the scheduled and structured arrangement. The ready availability of a few trained couples to care for those situations resolves this difficulty.

Several recent diocesan marital policies reflect this mandatory, but open and flexible approach.

In one diocese there is a regulation that the marriage preparation should begin with the proper minister one year prior to the wedding date. But the rule also states that it admits of flexibility for a reasonable cause, if in the prudent judgment of the pastoral minister the marriage preparation can be adequately completed.

In another diocese the minimum age for marriage has been elevated to 19 for good reasons, but it provides options for those under 19 or even 18.

The letter from the sailor in California which opened Chapter 3 illustrated the harmful effect of too rigidly applying a wise policy.

During the initial interview, the priest or deacon should not attempt to cover too much. It would be more important for him, after establishing the rapport we have discussed, simply to explain to the couple the various alternatives open to them and to arrange a preparation program that best fits their needs and availabilities.

Pope John Paul II curiously blends this notion of an obligatory, but open and flexible marriage preparation policy. He states that while "one must not underestimate the necessity and obligation of the immediate preparation for marriage... nevertheless such preparation must always be set forth and put into practice in such a way that omitting it is not an impediment to the celebration of marriage."[3]

We would hope that at the end of the initial interview the couple would walk away elated by the reception they have received and excited by the possibilities before them, rather than deflated by judgmental questions or crushed by complicated regulations.

6. *Assist the couple in reading a judgment about the existence and level of their own faith.*

The sacraments are actions of faith; they require and presuppose faith. There must be present, consequently, a certain minimal level of faith for a marriage to be celebrated in the Church.

This recommendation, however, states that the priest or deacon is not to judge about the existence or level of the engaged couple's faith, but to assist them in making their own judgment about that matter. They do, according to traditional Catholic teaching, minister the sacrament to one another. It is for them, therefore, to wrestle with that issue under the guidance of the clergy.

The pastor, to be sure, must oversee the situation and verify that the conditions for a valid and licit celebration are present. He also must be assured that a minimal faith exists in at least one of the parties.

But the clergy's role in marriage preparation is more of the facilitator than a judge, more of a wise guide than a judicial figure, more of an enlightening educator than an enforcing official. Acting as judge or enforcer with marginally Catholic couples has become an oppressive burden for many clergy. I hope a different understanding of their role will relieve them of needless worry and anxiety.

Our particular recommendation here enjoys the explicit backing of the official Church decrees we cited in the last chapter.

Pope John Paul II observed that couples seeking marriage in the Church possess faith in varying degrees and that the Church celebrates the marriages of those who are imperfectly disposed. He describes the kind of minimal faith required for the sacrament and for marriage in the Church: A couple who decide to marry according to the divine plan of committing their whole lives "in unbreakable love and unconditional faithfulness by an irrevocable nuptial consent," are reflecting, even if not in a fully conscious way, an attitude of profound obedience to God's will that cannot exist without God's grace.[4] The presence of such a decision, commitment and attitude means that they possess a seminal and sufficient, although perhaps only semiconscious faith.

The pontiff asserts that with such a choice or consent, the couple have entered upon a journey toward salvation, a journey which with their upright intention and through the immediate preparation and celebration of the sacrament can be complemented and brought to salvation. He reminds us that engaged couples, by baptism, already really share in Christ's marriage covenant with the Church.

The baptized couple (or person in an interreligious relationship) who possess the right intention described above have thus
accepted God's plan for marriage, consent at lest implicitly to what
the Church intends to do when she celebrates the exchange of nuptial vows and would seem to have sufficient faith for the sacrament
of matrimony.

These notions and their application reflect the principle of
compassion, mercy and forgiveness we have enunciated throughout this book.

The pope in the same document cited touches on an extremely
critical point. "As for wishing to lay down further criteria for admission to the ecclesial celebration of marriage, criteria that would
concern the level of faith of those to be married, this would above
all involve grave risks. In the first place, the risk of making unfounded and discriminatory judgments...."

Insistence on Sunday Mass attendance, formal parish registration and other similar behavioral patterns, however desirable in
themselves, would seem to fit into this category of "further criteria."

In summary, the very fact that a baptized couple appear at the
door and wish to be married in the Church, perhaps for only social
motives (e.g., "Our parents want this"), is not adequate reason to
move ahead with the celebration of the sacrament. But if they are
baptized *and* intend to marry according to the divine plan as explained above, the engaged pair possess the minimal requirements
for marriage in the Church, providing, of course, there exist no
major impediments.

Once again we are discussing minimal requirements, not ideal
expectations. The Holy Father reminds pastors that it is their duty
to promote such idealism by seeking to "facilitate a rediscovering,
nourishing and maturing" of the couple's faith which may be imperfect, weak and barely alive. The *Code of Canon Law,* in its terse
way, also portrays those desired ideals, but without making them
essential requirements. Catholics not yet confirmed are to receive
that sacrament, it states, "If they can do it without serious inconvenience" (Canon 1065:1). Moreover, "it is strongly recommended

that those to be married approach the sacraments of penance and the Most Holy Eucharist so they may fruitfully receive the sacrament of marriage" (Canon 1065:2).

Receiving the sacrament validly and licitly is one issue; doing so fruitfully is another. Upholding the ideal is one task of the clergy and pastoral ministers; requiring the minimal is quite another.

I have found that concern about the faith of couples who seek marriage is one of the most perplexing and troublesome challenges the clergy and their pastoral associates face in parishes today. It is my hope that this book, this chapter and this recommendation will reduce some of those pressing anxieties. It is also my wish that the following recommendation will lighten an equally heavy burden — the clergy's worry over a couple's readiness to marry, their compatibility with each other and the prospects they have for a successful marriage.

7. *Assist the couple in reading a judgment about their basic readiness for marriage.*

As a priest who has served in pastoral ministry for over 40 years, I today experience occasional bittersweet encounters with persons for whom I was the officiating priest at their marriages long ago. The sweet, joyful moments are chance or planned meetings with people who have celebrated, for example, their silver anniversaries and recall my presence at their wedding when we were all younger.

The bitter, sad moments are with people whose marriages turned sour and ended in divorce. There is usually some awkwardness in those visits, especially the brief and chance ones. How do you express in a few moments to a priest who knew you at a different time, place and space the experiences of dashed dreams, the death of a relationship, the misunderstandings and hurts which led to separation and divorce, the later false starts or harmful compensatory behavior, the possible alienation from God and the Church, the remarriage for a second or third time, the complexity of single parenthood or blended families and all the other complications which occur in 20 to 30 years of real living? And how does a priest respond in such a short encounter with empathy and compassion to the intense outpouring of openly expressed or obviously suppressed feelings?

Fortunately for me, and I believe for most clergy in similar situations, I tend neither to take the credit for the successful unions nor to shoulder the blame for the failed ones. Still, the sadness about the broken unions does seem to outweigh the joy over the healthy bonds.

The high rate of divorce in this country with its companion negative effects, obvious from our own experiences and verified by statistics, has prompted Church leaders to establish various restrictive requirements for marriage like waiting periods, mandatory classes and assessment processes. The purpose is noble: By making it harder to marry in the Church, we should be able to stem the flood of divorces or at least help many couples avoid the horrendous pains of a marital disruption. While we cannot measure how effective these steps have been, it appears reasonable to conclude that by forcing engaged couples to look seriously at their relationship and at marriage itself these policies have led some to abort their plans or to enter the marital state with more mature awareness and deeper commitment.

But these well-meaning procedures have produced some seriously destructive side effects as well.

First of all, they run perilously close to violating the couple's natural right to marry. Dominican David O'Rourke, in commenting on the assessment processes designed to evaluate a couple's readiness for marriage, warns, "I do not think I am exaggerating in saying that if this kind of assessment process were used to establish the right to vote it would be challenged for being as discriminatory as the poll tax and as arbitrary as the literacy test."[5] His experience and competence in the marriage preparation and enrichment field give that admonition weight even beyond its intrinsic worth.

Second, and this is connected with O'Rourke's observation,

the presumption rests on an extremely fragile base that anyone — priest, deacon, pastoral minister or sponsor couple — can make an assessment about the couple's readiness for marriage or predict the future of their marital relationship.

A priest confessor, also a psychologist, does extensive testing of candidates for the religious life and serves as a consultant for our diocesan marriage tribunal. The man states quite frankly that he cannot predict the successful futures of clients, but he can predict with moral certitude their forthcoming failures.

An author of one of the premarital discussion instruments maintains that there are no means to evaluate the possibility of a couple making their marriage successful, because it is not possible to measure future potential.

Our own pastoral and personal experiences can give countless testimonies of surprises, of marriages "made in heaven" that did not work and dubious couplings of people who are presently preparing for their golden anniversaries. Those surprises extend to the preparation procedures as well. I know of and am sure other clergy could name couples who completed with conscientiousness and enthusiasm all the suggested steps to prepare for marriage and yet who separated before a decade passed. Conversely, I and other clergy could name couples whose participation in the marital preparation programs was reluctant and spotty, but whose subsequent marriages have been strong and steady.

The point here is not at all to downplay the value of these programs, but simply to indicate that projecting or predicting the future based upon them is a near impossibility.

In this context we must also mention the ever possible and always present power of grace. In Chapter 2, we described the journey of a Christian as uniquely personal, uneven and lifelong. That holds true for a marital relationship as well. Grace can and does work wonders, often in hidden and surprising ways.

Making assessments and projections about a person or a couple's future is terribly risky and a very unstable basis for an institutional policy.

Third, such procedures indirectly place a heavy burden upon the pastor and/or the priest or deacon who presides at the celebration as well as upon those involved in marriage preparation procedures. It is not, in the light of those procedures, sufficient for these people to ask themselves: "Did we warmly welcome the couple? Did we teach the ideal? Did we offer them a solid, yet flexible preparation course? Did we help them to prepare and to celebrate a faith-filled, prayerful nuptial liturgy?" They may instead pose to themselves much harder and truly unfair questions: "Will their marriage work? Why didn't it succeed? Should we have foreseen the problem? Is it my or our fault?"

The first battery of inquiries is appropriate and useful; the second is not. We are responsible for the teaching and the guidance, not the response and the outcome.

Fourth and finally, these procedures enter into the judgment-making arena. Pope John Paul II, as we have just noted, explicitly cautions against "further criteria for admission to the ecclesial celebration of marriage" because this "involves the grave risk of making unfounded and discriminatory judgments." If he warns us about making such judgments concerning the level of faith of the couple, how much greater caution must we exercise about making judgments concerning the far more elusive issue of a couple's readiness for marriage and the future of their relationship.

The Church does require that the pastor or his delegate make some judgments, but they are more of an external or negative nature. We must see to it that nothing stands in the way of a valid and licit celebration. Major impediments (e.g., previous marriage, serious psychological immaturity, need for dispensations, under age) must be cleared away. If serious obstacles persist the bishop can prohibit their marriage, but even he may do so only for a time and for a serious cause and solely for as long as that cause exists. Nevertheless, the Church does not demand that the pastor or his delegate move beyond these fundamentally negative and essentially external judgments.

We return to the theological truth that the bride and groom

minister the sacrament to one another. Should they not also be the persons to judge their readiness to receive this gift?

The archdiocese and dioceses in the state of Missouri have established a Common Marriage Policy which appears to endorse that concept and our recommendation. One goal for marriage preparation, according to that document, is to provide a framework within which "the couple has the best possible opportunity to assess their individual readiness to marry."

The Church's role as well as the primary task of clergy and others in marriage preparation, it seems, is to assist the couple in making a judgment both about their relational readiness and personal faith, not to make those judgments for or about them.

8. *Involve lay persons in the marriage preparation programs.*

In Chapter 8 we outlined the theological and practical support official Church documents give to the involvement of lay persons in baptismal preparation programs. Those comments apply in parallel fashion to the sacrament of matrimony. Moreover, the last chapter cited texts which specifically endorse and urge the use of lay people for marriage preparation efforts.

However, in addition to the inherent value of this "like to like" ministry which we described in connection with baptism, there is the model and hope which a well-adjusted, successfully married couple offer to the engaged pair. Because of today's pervasive atmosphere of marital misery, divorce and lack of commitment, the bride and groom-to-be often worry about whether they too will become another negative statistic. Encountering the example of a happy, content and loving veteran husband and wife bolsters their hopes and dissipates some of those worries.

Moreover, the spouses' love for God, dedication to the Church and active practice of the faith, qualities which flow from and also fuel their caring marital bond, silently say something to the engaged couple.

The marriage preparation program of a large suburban parish in Arizona illustrated this desired active involvement of lay persons who are collaboratively working with the clergy in the marriage preparation ministry.[6]

Because it is a popular place for weddings and many couples from outside the area seek to be married there, the pastor requires parish registration before making initial arrangements. Since they average nearly 100 marriages annually, the church has for efficiency's sake prepared an informational booklet answering most of the practical questions an engaged pair normally ask. The parish secretary gives this to the inquiring couple and at the same time establishes an appointment for them with the priest.

During that first interview the clergyman gets to know the couple and explains the marital instrument FOCCUS. The prospective bride and groom then come to the rectory at their convenience during a subsequent weekday (Monday-Saturday, 8:30 a.m. to 9:00 p.m.) and spend 45 minutes completing the FOCCUS questionnaire. A staff member graphs the results and the couple are requested to call three days afterwards for an appointment with the priest to review the results of their experience with FOCCUS.

The priest may have three to six sessions with the couple discussing the agreements and disagreements, likes and dislikes, similarities and differences between the two of them which emerge from the FOCCUS results and appear on the graph.

The pair then take part in a six-session "Evenings for the Engaged," normally with four or five other couples planning marriage. Four married couples handle the coordination and presentations of these evenings as well as host them in their homes on a rotating basis. The priest comes to the final session, presents a theology of marriage, celebrates a Eucharist for the group and shares a potluck supper with all.

The couple return then for another session with the priest who will preside at their wedding. They evaluate their participation in "Evenings for the Engaged" (90 percent are enthusiastic about them). The priest gives the couple a personalized plaque with their names and the date of their wedding inscribed upon it. He also offers them the option of making an Engaged Encounter. Most are not familiar with this weekend experience and few take advantage of that alternative. At this session he also supplies them with the booklet, *Together for Life,* and outlines the liturgical possibilities for them as described in that text.

They return later with their choices for the liturgy and walk through the ceremony as they have designed it with the presider. Following this, they meet the parish wedding hostess who will assist them during the rehearsal and at the liturgy itself. There are four parishioners trained for that function and they receive a modest offering.

9. Make use of the liturgical preparation and celebration as teachable and touchable moments.

While couples generally are pleased with marriage preparation programs of whatever nature, their primary desire and focus is to get married and to have a beautiful wedding ceremony. At the onset, the marital preparatory steps we offer, however open and flexible, frequently may be viewed by the engaged couple merely as steps they must go through in order to have a Church marriage.

That makes the preparation and celebration of the liturgy what I would term both teachable and touchable moments. We are familiar enough with the teachable moment concept connected with first penance, Eucharist and confirmation. We use these high interest opportunities to teach the parents, other adults and candidates some central truths about the faith. But those are also touchable moments. They are significant occasions, and the same people want to connect with God during them to express their joys, to be comforted in their sorrows, to discover guidance amidst their confusion, to gain strength for their burdens and to build up hope in tomorrow. If teachable moments address the head with religious information, touchable moments move the heart with spiritual inspiration.

All of these notions apply with special force to the sacrament of matrimony and its preparation and celebration. The official directives of the Church quoted in the last chapter explicitly mention how they can be very important for the discovery and strengthening of the bride and groom's faith.

Here are a few suggestions for facilitating the preparation and celebration of the nuptial liturgy:

• I personally prefer giving the couple a book like my own *Together for Life* during the initial interview.[7] In that way they receive a free gift at the very start; they can see in concrete fashion the great freedom and rich opportunities open to them, catch at their leisure a few comments about marriage, and early on begin to read biblical texts about marriage.

When I wrote the comments accompanying the texts 25 years and nearly eight million copies ago, I simply put down ideas I had tried to communicate in person to engaged couples throughout the first dozen years of my priestly ministry. These commentaries were not meant to constitute a series of biblical explanations, but to form a simplified, succinct marriage preparation course.

A brief explanation can show how the couple could use this text both as a vehicle for building better communication and for praying together in a biblically reflective manner.

• Involvement of various persons as readers, gift bearers, etc. has now become commonplace. We might keep in mind here two principles: The *process* of using relatives or friends is highly desirable, but in roles such as proclaiming the Word or providing the music, a certain emphasis on the quality of the *product* needs to be maintained. Otherwise, poor reading of scripture or rendering of the music will mar the liturgical celebration.

• There are several ways to involve the parents in an active way: by encouraging a more creative entrance procession in which both parents participate; by inviting them to bring up the gifts; by offering them the occasion to make a few remarks to the couple as part of the homily (I witnessed this effectively done in the African Kingdom of Lesotho in the 1970's) or after communion (by analogy to the revised funeral rite); by incorporating their personal ideas into the preacher's homily; by bringing them forward to lay hands on their daughter or son at the last blessing.

• A competent parish *music director* can contribute greatly by meeting personally with the couple beforehand to discuss possibilities. He or she can expand their vision of suitable music ("No, the theme music from *Jaws* isn't really an appropriate responsorial psalm and 'The First Time I Lay Beside You' wouldn't do well as a communion piece"), happily combine their wishes with good sacred compositions, and promote congregational singing at the liturgy.

• While the Church explicitly holds up the ideal of celebrating marriage within Mass, there are many reasons why more and more of our nuptial liturgies will be done outside Mass. In some circumstances, such as an interreligious marriage, that option may even be the preferred alternative.

• There no longer exists the obligation to give a set number of instructions about the Church to a partner who is not Catholic in a forthcoming interreligious marriage. Offering that option, however, could prove pastorally effective for a variety of reasons.[8]

• The idea of a wedding host or hostess or *rehearsal coordinator* has great merit, particularly for parishes with a great number of weddings. Nevertheless, the rehearsal is one of those high-risk moments, filled with potential for good or harm. I recall years ago a wise mentor saying, "Be patient at rehearsals: If you are, they will never forget you; if you are not, they will never forgive you." A mix of persons and functions might be in order here. The presider could greet the wedding party, meet all of them, create a pleasant atmosphere, lead them in a brief prayer service (quieting down, a passage from scripture like one of John's texts from the ritual on love, a spontaneous prayer by the priest or deacon and an Our Father) and then turn the rest of the rehearsal over to the coordinator who would take them through the time and energy-consuming practice of the ceremony itself.

• When there is time, I have found that the rehearsal dinner is an excellent occasion to visit with the parents, draw from them a few reflections on marriage, learn a bit about their own backgrounds and discover who are some of the expected out-of-town guests. That information proves useful the next day in greeting the assembly and as part of the homily itself.

• There are numerous other creative ways in which the clergy in our times attempt to make the wedding ceremony a joyous and inspiring event for the bride and groom as well as for the assembled guests. What we hope to accomplish is to leave them with a positive memory of their experience with the Church at this momentous occasion in their lives. Later, as they mature and as their values shift, those warm recollections may prompt a return to Church for renewing and deepening their faith.

10. *Support married couples afterwards and help heal the brokenhearted.*

Pope John Paul II considers "aftercare" a part of the entire marriage preparation process. He sees this as a responsibility of the entire Church community. In particular, he recognizes the needs of young families who are especially vulnerable, "in the first years of marriage, to possible difficulties such as those created by adaptation to life together or by the birth of children."[9]

Empirical data confirm his observation. Some 50 percent of all divorces occur during the first five years of married life and 33 percent of all separations happen within two years.

The Hartford archdiocese conducted a pilot counseling referral project as a response to this phenomenon and challenge. During the marriage preparation program, engaged couples are introduced and speak with professional counselors on the archdiocesan staff. The couples are then encouraged, when significant difficulties arise in the first years of married life, to make contact with this counselor who can facilitate their own dialogue and help them resolve conflicts in constructive fashion.

Some parish priests attempt to keep in contact through cards or calls with the couples at whose marriages they have presided, but sheer numbers and changes of address make that a rather awesome task.

While the Church has not yet really developed comprehensive programs to promote the aftercare of married couples, blame for that weakness should not be totally placed at the feet of diocesan or parish family life leadership. In many or most instances, young and newlywed married persons have quite a different agenda before them. Their careers, homes and adjustments tend to take precedence over Church involvement.

Nevertheless, parishes often can and do reach out to young married couples through targeted homilies, hospitality groups, invitations to share their diverse talents with the community, encouragement of enrichment experiences like Marriage Encounter and celebration of anniversaries. A particularly effective method is the active recruitment of young couples for service in the marriage preparation ministry. They can thus help others as they were helped themselves.

We could see such support of married couples as the positive dimension of aftercare. But there is, unfortunately, the need for the critical aspect of aftercare which reaches out to troubled marriages and tries to help heal those brokenhearted by separation or divorce.

The death of a marital relationship is a devastating experience. In many cases the affected person frequently feels abandoned by the Church or abandons it. The clergy and pastoral ministers need to be particularly sensitive to this and provide remedies for that trend.

Parish or regional divorce and separated groups help. So do sensitive homilies which uphold the dignity of marriage, but simultaneously explain correctly the status of the divorced and give them hope for the future. So, too, will a keen awareness of the plight of single parents which leads to invitations for them to take an active part in parish life through such simple actions as bringing up the gifts at Sunday Mass.

The Church favors marriage in its law and in case of doubt the validity of a marriage is upheld.[10] At the same time it provides relief and an opportunity for a new start in the case of those whose marriages lacked an essential element from the beginning. The marital tribunal procedures in most dioceses of the United States are admirable in this regard. They are thorough, but sensitive and pastoral in their style and reasonable in cost, time and mechanics. We need, however, a standardization of that phenomenon throughout the nation to avoid inequities in treatment.

Given the contemporary forces which militate against lasting marital bonds, it is essential that we have helpful parish and diocesan procedures and personnel to assist those nearly destroyed by the breakdown and breakup of their marriage relationships. These people are anxious to be healed and eager to move on with their lives.

Conclusion

Priests, deacons and pastoral ministers need to challenge, but not crush those who come to them seeking the sacraments and services of the Church.

They need to be at one and the same time both teachers and shepherds, simultaneously holding up the ideal, while reaching out to marginal Catholics.

They need to be prophets proclaiming God's message with consistency, truth and courage, yet searching for stray members with compassion, mercy and forgiveness.

In preaching the demands of justice and holiness, they need, above all, to be like their Master, the suffering servant Messiah, extremely careful not to break the bruised reed or to snuff out the smoldering wick.

Guidance from the *Catechism*

Article 1621: "In the Latin Rite the celebration of marriage between two Catholic faithful normally takes place during Holy Mass, because of the connection of all the sacraments with the Paschal mystery of Christ (cf. *SC* 61). In the Eucharist the memorial of the New Covenant is realized, the New Covenant in which Christ has united himself forever to the Church, his beloved bride for whom he gave himself up (cf. *LG* 6). It is therefore fitting that the spouses should seal their consent to give themselves to each other through the offering of their own lives by uniting it to the offering of Christ for his Church made present in the Eucharistic sacrifice, and by receiving the Eucharist so that, communicating in the same Body and the same Blood of Christ, they may form but 'one body' in Christ" (cf. *1 Cor* 10:17).

Article 1632: "So that the 'I do' of the spouses may be a free and responsible act and so that the marriage covenant may have solid and lasting human and Christian foundations, preparation for marriage is of prime importance.

The example and teaching given by parents and families remain the special form of this preparation.

The role of pastors and of the Christian community as the 'family of God' is indispensable for the transmission of the human and Christian values of marriage and family (cf. CIC, can. 1063), and much more so in our era when many young people experience broken homes which no longer sufficiently assure this initiation:

> It is imperative to give suitable and timely instruction to young people, above all in the heart of their own families, about the dignity of married love, its role and its exercise, so that, having learned the value of chastity, they will be able at a suitable age to engage in honorable courtship and enter upon a marriage of their own" (*GS* 49 §3).

Article 1641: "'By reason of their state in life and of their order, [Christian spouses] have their own special gifts in the People of God' (*LG* 11 §2). This grace proper to the sacrament of Matrimony is intended to perfect the couple's love and to strengthen their indissoluble unity. By this grace they 'help one another to attain holiness in their married life and in welcoming and educating their children'" (*LG* 11 §2; cf. *LG* 41).

Article 1642: "'…Just as of old God encountered this people with a covenant of love and fidelity, so our Savior, the spouse of the Church, now encounters Christian spouses through the sacrament of Matrimony' (*GS* 48 §2). Christ dwells with them, gives them the strength to take up their crosses and so follow him, to rise again after they have fallen, to forgive one another, to bear one another's burdens, to 'be subject to one another out of reverence for Christ' (*Eph* 5:21; cf. *Gal* 6:2), and to love one another with supernatural, tender, and fruitful love.…'"

Concluding Summary

*W*e have summarized below the main points of each chapter in this book for readers who wish to gain a general overview of its content or seek to review rather swiftly the essential message of each section, particularly Chapters 1-6.

1. Categorizing people as marginal Catholics is a risky, questionable, elusive and complex procedure. It involves making judgments which only God can and may do. It also necessarily requires using certain external, religious behavioral patterns as criteria for measuring the existence or level of a person's inner, spiritual faith. But today those observable measurements for Catholics are not as clear and defined as in yesteryear; moreover, there has never been an automatic or perfect connection between peoples' surface actions and their interior attitudes. Having issued those disclaimers and cautions, we define, in the context and for the purpose of this book's discussion, marginal Catholics as those who, for any one of several reasons, possess only a tenuous connection with the parish. Because of that weak link, these persons pose a challenge to the clergy and pastoral leaders when they seek a sacrament or service of the Church.

2. The spiritual path of a Christian is an ongoing, uneven and lifelong journey. It includes repeated conversions or turning points during which we move from one attitude or status to another. It takes on the character of a highly individualized and unpredictable process. Consequently, pastoral ministers need respect and patience in responding to the persons whom they serve. They must respect

the Holy Spirit's gentle, often surprising and hidden movements within hearts. They must wait with patience, since journeys of faith proceed at their own frequently slow pace and usually cannot be hurried. Four Church resources support both this analysis of the conversion process phenomenon and the desired pastoral response to it: the *Rite of Christian Initiation of Adults*, adult faith development theories, a comparison with the stages of grief, and several statistical surveys about the religious practices of young Catholics from their teens to late twenties.

3. The Old Testament portrays a jealous God who seemingly does not tolerate marginal followers or lukewarm believers. It notes, however, that this same God is slow to anger and rich in kindness toward those who repent of their infidelity. Moreover, it points to the future and promised Messiah as a suffering servant or potter working with clay who will take a more gentle and quiet approach to those who refuse or are reluctant to accept and follow his message. The New Testament offers Jesus as the awaited one who fulfills the earlier prophecies. He will be a patient Savior bringing pardon and showing great care lest he break the bruised reed or quench the smoldering wick. Christ's parables about the wheat and the weeds, the net full of fish and the lost sheep, coin or son likewise underscore the importance of practicing patience with those who fail to live up perfectly to his teaching.

4. The Catholic Church, because of its constant upholding of absolute truths or principles on the world level and because of its occasional rigid pastoral practice on the parish level, is viewed by some today as harsh and cruel, not compassionate and forgiving. Overzealous insistence on firm and personal commitment to the Church, concerns about the need of a live faith as a requisite for reception of the sacraments and a weakening of belief in the power of the sacramental rite itself are factors leading to procedures which can appear as severe and inflexible. Official Church documents and the reflections of certain Catholic scholars urge several points: a blend of consistency and truth in teaching with compassion and

mercy in pastoral practice; a mix of belief in the risen Christ's presence and power in the sacraments with the acceptance of the need for a participant's faith and understanding to make these sacraments fruitful or effective; a recognition that the Church is a community of different disciples, of saints and sinners, of hot, lukewarm and cold followers of Christ. The Church, then, is a "messy," not an "elitist" body, always posing the ideal for its members, but able to accept them in their weakness where they are.

5. The secular and the sacred or Church legal systems, among other things, agree on these two points: that laws are good and even necessary for every society; but all laws, as products of limited, flawed and changing human minds and circumstances are imperfect and can never adequately cover every individual case or situation. Secular law in the United States follows the English or Anglo-Saxon legal system with complex legislation touching on very specific details and admitting of few or no exceptions. Church law is based on the European or Roman legal system which features fewer and more general norms with interpretation, adaptation or exceptions an understood part of that arrangement. The tendency of American Catholics to interpret Church law as strictly as they do secular law can cause tensions and sometimes needless problems. Church law implements the principle of consistency and truth through a code of diverse legislation with variable binding obligations which sketch and promote the ideals of Christian living. However, it implements the principle of compassion and mercy by providing legal exceptions, adaptations, exemptions and interpretations such as dispensations, excusing causes and *epieikeia.* The principle of consistency requires that deviations from Church law not be done lightly or without proportionate reason. The principle of compassion requires that pastoral leaders, especially the clergy, apply the principles of Church law in an informed and benign way to particular cases.

6. The initial meetings between clergy or pastoral ministers and persons who seek the sacraments or services of the Church are

high-risk encounters. The many conscious and unconscious factors making this a particularly sensitive moment for the petitioners include awkwardness caused by the unfamiliar nature of the experience, often hidden or overt mistrust or resentment of religious authorities, anxiety heightened by unusual circumstances, negative attitudes caused by past burdens, preoccupation with external concerns, and uncomfortableness with the prospect of a new set of human relationships. The interviewing clergy or pastoral ministers are influenced by many of those same elements, but they also need to ask themselves a series of reflective questions to determine what may be the motivating influence behind their response to those who approach them. For the best interaction in these situations, Church leaders should try to conduct personal, not telephone or written interviews, avoid a defensiveness in the face of expressed contrary values or practices, be positive as well as flexible, and arrange for no interruptions during the session. These are opportunities for evangelization in which the clergy, especially, as servants of truth and consistency, but animated by love, extend a warm, gracious hospitality to all.

7. The Church's official directives for baptism have been excerpted from three Vatican documents: The 1969 *Rite of Baptism for Children*, a 1980 *Instruction on Infant Baptism*, and the 1983 *Code of Canon Law*. With regard to baptizing the children of marginally Catholic parents, these texts offer two great principles, the second of which is subordinate to the first. The first proclaims the dignity of baptism, its necessity for salvation, its nature as a gift from God through the Church, and the caution that this sacrament with its effects upon infants must not be delayed. The second stresses the requirement for assurances that the gift thus granted will bear fruit through the child's authentic education in Christian faith and practice. With regard to parents who have little faith and practice their religion only occasionally, the decrees require a well-founded hope that the baptized child will receive a Christian upbringing. Any pledge giving that type of hope, however, deserves to be considered

as sufficient. In all cases the pastor or his delegate needs to enter into clear-sighted and understanding dialogue with the parents about these matters.

8. Ten pastoral suggestions flow from the ideas in Chapters 1-6; they correspond to the Church's official directives outlined in Chapter 7 and represent procedures practiced by many clergy in the United States and Canada. Among those recommendations are the following: Teach the ideal; insist, but with flexibility, on parental participation in some sort of educational and formational preparation; encourage parish affiliation or registration, but do not mandate reception or use of parish envelopes as a requisite for baptism; avoid making Mass attendance a requirement for baptism; treat each request for baptism on an individual basis according to the general Church principles outlined in Chapter 7; and delay, never refuse baptism.

9. The Church's official directives for marriage have also been excerpted from three Vatican documents: the 1969 *Rite of Marriage*, the 1981 Apostolic Exhortation *On the Family* by Pope John Paul II and the 1983 *Code of Canon Law*. The Church, upholding the natural right of couples to marry, instructs pastors to go ahead with marriage in the Church if all requirements for a valid and licit ceremony have been fulfilled. Faith upon the part of at least one of the engaged pair is essential, but the Church does witness the marriages of those whose faith is imperfect or minimal. There are two basic requisites for marriage in the Church beyond those which affect the valid and licit nature of the celebration. First, the couple must intend even in an unconscious way to marry according to God's plan, i.e., to give a consent to one another which is irrevocable, exclusive and life-lasting. Such a promise cannot be done without grace and consequently such an intention indicates the presence of a seminal and sufficient faith for the sacrament. Second, the couple, or at least one member, must be baptized in the Church. Further, external criteria for determining the existence or level of faith in the engaged couple are risky and to be avoided, especially because they involve

making ill-founded judgments. The Church urges a suitable preparation program and appropriate liturgical celebration to insure that the sacrament will bear fruit.

10. Ten pastoral suggestions for marriage, in parallel fashion to those for baptism, flow from the ideas in Chapters 1-6; they correspond to the Church's official directives outlined in Chapter 9 and represent procedures practiced by many clergy in the United States and Canada. Among these recommendations are the following: Use marital instruments or inventories as tools to promote dialogue, not as tests to measure a couple's readiness for marriage; insist, but in a flexible and open manner, upon some form of marriage preparation program; assist the couple in reaching their own judgments about the existence and level of their own faith and their readiness for marriage; don't require regular Mass attendance as an essential condition for marriage in the Church; use the preparation and celebration of the nuptial liturgy as a teachable and touchable moment for the couple; support married couples afterwards; and, finally, help heal those brokenhearted by marital disruptions.

Process and
Acknowledgments

This book grew out of a sabbatical opportunity and a pastoral need.

Our diocese of Syracuse in New York has developed in the past decades an excellent policy of clergy sabbaticals. Priests may take from three months to a year away from their assigned duties depending on the length of time they have served in the active ministry. In the early '80's I had been thinking about a six-month sabbatical, perhaps combining some study of Scripture in the Holy Land with a few theology courses in Rome. Then Father Charles Gusmer, a long-time colleague and resident liturgist at the Darlington Seminary in New Jersey, suggested that with my background in pastoral writing and speaking, I should seek a full year's leave for this purpose and probably could find a college or university which would welcome me as a resident lecturer. Another friend, Father Frank McNulty, supported this idea and generously offered to help with arrangements.

Their encouragement prompted me to take steps which could turn the vague dream into a specific reality. I applied for the sabbatical according to our diocesan procedures and Bishop Frank J. Harrison through his personnel director, Rev. George F. Sheehan, granted me leave from September 1987 to June 1988. Later, when another responsibility and a heavy schedule of speaking engagements slowed down this project about marginal Catholics, Bishop Harrison's successor, Most Rev. Joseph T. O'Keefe, extended the sabbatical until May 1989.

Over the past quarter of a century, I have addressed about 30,000 priests through 75 clergy retreats and countless clerical conferences. In addition, my more than two million miles of lecture travel, mostly in the United States and Canada but also in a few places abroad, have put me in contact with many religious and lay people deeply concerned about the Church. Throughout the past two decades especially, I have heard at those retreats and conferences, during exchanges at lectures, and in personal conversations, repeated surfacing of the issues treated in this book. "How do we respond to parents who seek baptism for their children, but do not go to church?" and "How do we react to couples who want a Church wedding, but seldom, or never, go to Mass?" These were not academic questions or neutral discussions. Participants quickly would cite recent real cases of these dilemmas and often would express intense feelings of anger, frustration or worry about what they did or did not do in given situations.

In our diocese, for example, the Senate of Priests asked the diocesan cabinet to prepare for the bishop guidelines which he would issue to cover these matters. Part of their desire was to bring about a certain uniformity. Priests and pastoral ministers in parishes with mandated baptismal classes, for example, were annoyed to learn that the neighboring Catholic church down the street did not require such sessions. Rules from the bishop would resolve that problem or at least provide official support for parish procedures.

But I think that part of the reason for this request for rules was to remove from the clergy the anxious burden of deciding whether or not to baptize a particular child or to officiate at a particular couple's wedding. Those who have persevered through this book should understand that neither the universal Church legislation nor diocesan issued norms will fulfill that desire. The pastorally wise Church leaves the ultimate decision for each case in the hands of the pastor or his delegate. At the same time, faithful readers will, I hope, have discovered that such a responsibility, when properly understood, is less onerous than many priests make it out to be.

In any event, determining the best way of reaching out to marginal Catholics, particularly in connection with baptism and marriage, was and continues to be a keenly felt pastoral need.

My initial notion of this combined sabbatical opportunity and pastoral project was, first, to read around the subject under the guidance of recognized scholars in the biblical, theological, liturgical, legal and pastoral fields, an enterprise which would be for my own enrichment as well as for necessary research; second, to survey in some way clergy, religious and lay people about this issue for their input; third, to write a book for clergy, pastoral ministers and others interested which would contain the fruit of my study and offer practical suggestions for dealing with these requests from marginal Catholics.

The completion of this book, indicates that my three goals have been achieved. As in all human endeavors, however, the plan of action shifted on various occasions for different reasons.

My original concept was to locate for several months each in university settings in East Coast, Midwest and West Coast areas. During this early stage of planning, many people were wonderfully generous in making recommendations, volunteering assistance or referring me to appropriate persons. Father Robert Pelton, C.S.C., of Notre Dame's Institute for Clergy Education supported the idea and put me in touch with David C. Leege, then Professor of Government at Notre Dame's Center for the Study of Contemporary Society. Despite his busy occupation with the Notre Dame Study of Catholic Parish Life, Leege sent me a lengthy letter with excellent suggestions. Father Richard McBrien, also of Notre Dame, was most cooperative in providing data about the possibility of being a residential scholar at my alma mater. My thought was to drive on weekends to parishes near the three university locations and to gather information there from personnel at those churches, thus giving me a national sampling of parish situations.

Professor Leege recommended I contact Dr. Francis J. Butler in Washington, the president of FADICA (Foundations and Donors Interested in Catholic Activities), about the possibility of a grant to cover expenses during the research and writing. At Butler's instigation, Father Philip Murnion of the National Pastoral Life Center in New York City, with the help of staff person Sister Mary Ann Barnhorn, S.N.D., sent applications to several foundations and potential donors.

As the months passed, prospects for a grant seemed dim. Without such funding, I consequently decided to alter my plan. Instead of staying at three university locations, I would continue to reside at St. Joseph's Parish in Camillus, New York, and accept more than my usual amount of speaking engagements. This would get me around the country at no cost and enable me to gather input in that fashion.

The tactic worked well, even if it did create a demanding schedule and cut into reading, research and writing time. During the September-June 1987 period, I touched base with over 100 clergy and many religious in more than 20 archdioceses and dioceses. These included Tulsa, Denver, Jackson, St. Augustine, Dubuque, Green Bay, Phoenix, Erie, Chicago, Joliet, Toronto, Covington, Kansas City in Kansas, Dallas, San Diego, St. Petersburg, Los Angeles, Orange, Bismarck, Metuchen, Portland in Maine, Buffalo, Crookston and Winona. I am most grateful for those people who welcomed me and shared their insights.

As the sabbatical year began and developed, I tested a few of the major results of my research mostly in clergy gatherings. Their always attentive and sometimes intense reactions verified that the need was, in fact, present and the involvement of clergy, highly personal. At these sessions there were opportunities for interaction and response, all of which proved very valuable to me. I extend my gratitude to those participants: the several dozen Air Force chaplains at Scottsdale, Arizona, at Vallembrosa, California, and at North Palm Beach, Florida; the members of the Vatican II Institute for Clergy Formation at Menlo Park, California; the diocesan clergy of Spokane, Washington, Bismarck, North Dakota, and Portland, Maine.

To my pleasant surprise, just prior to the official sabbatical beginning, I learned that Our Sunday Visitor Institute Advisory

Council approved the request for a grant. While my new plan did not make funding such a critical concern, I was, nevertheless, grateful for their support, a support liberal in the amount bestowed and even more liberal in the conditions attached to the grant. My thanks here to the administrator of the Institute, always gracious Dale Francis, and to the members of the Advisory Council. The National Pastoral Life Center administered the grant with Harry Fagan caring for the details. As the project unfolded, the importance of this grant became more and more evident and enabled me to complete it with much greater thoroughness than would otherwise have been possible.

My mentors were many and extended warm hospitality to me on every occasion. The footnotes mention some who made major contributions of time and energy such as Rev. Michael Beers, Rev. Raymond Brown, S.S., Rev. Avery Dulles, S.J., Professor Samuel J.M. Donnelly, Msgr. Frederick R. McManus, Rev. Patrick O'Leary and Rev. Neal Quartier. But there were many others. People such as an old and now deceased friend, Rev. Thomas J. McLaughlin, who mentioned *Once a Catholic* to me, Rev. Dennis J. Smolarski, S.J., who volunteered his time for a discussion on the liturgy, Rev. Stephen Rossetti, Rev. Darr Schoenhofen, Dr. Dean Hoge, Patricia Livingston, Rev. Joseph Ford, Most Rev. Joseph T. O'Keefe and James J. O'Connell.

My article in the January 31, 1988 issue of *Our Sunday Visitor* produced an unexpected windfall. Over 40 letters came in response to my invitation for accounts of being crushed or challenged in the past by the Church. They were personal and touching, and confirmed to me that this topic affects lay people as acutely as it does the clergy. Those that were the most articulate and pertinent introduce eight of the chapters in the book.

A book is better when competent, but constructive, critics review it for you in advance. My gratitude to them: Sister Charla Commins, C.S.J., Patricia Livingston, Rev. John Roark, Rev. John Catoir, Most Rev. Thomas J. Costello, Rev. Avery Dulles, S.J., Rev. Patrick O'Leary, Rev. Neal Quartier, Rev. Stephen Rossetti, Robert Fitzgerald, Rev. Michael Beers and Rev. Donald Krebs.

Father Phil Murnion and his associates at the National Pastoral Life Center aided, at the outset, in developing a few directions for me and were obviously helpful, as well, in securing and managing the grant. They also made good recommendations when the book was near completion as to its potential publisher.

Finally, this sabbatical opportunity and pastoral book would not have been possible without the able and conscientious assistance of my secretary-typist for ten years, Mrs. Patricia Gale. An IBM computer/word processor and the assistance of her retired husband, Art, have made a bit easier the task of translating my increasingly bad handscript into a readable manuscript. I am grateful to both of them and for the positive benefits of modern technology as well. My appreciation also to Robert Offerman for his assistance with the expensive duplication of materials required throughout the project.

Human weakness may have caused me to omit the acknowledgment of some persons who contributed to this project. If that be the case, I beg their forgiveness for such an oversight.

In grateful prayer, I ask God to bless those who made both this sabbatical and this book possible. In hopeful prayer, I ask God to bless all of the text's readers, that these pages may help both those who minister the sacraments and those who receive them to realize that Jesus ever challenges us to be more, but is always compassionate with us in our weakness.

NOTES

Chapter 1: Once a Catholic

1. Peter Occhiogrosso, *Once a Catholic* (Boston: Houghton Mifflin Company, 1987), p. 176.
2. *Ibid.,* pp. 216, 365.
3. *Origins,* Volume 18, No. 7, June 30, 1988, p. 100.
4. *The Inside Stories: 13 Valiant Women Challenging the Church,* edited by Annie Lally Muhaven (Mystic, CT: Twenty-Third Publications, 1987), pp. v, vii.
5. *Ibid.,* pp. 102, 120, 129, 156, 227-229, 238.
6. Charles E. Curran, *Faithful Dissent* (Kansas City, MO: Sheed & Ward, 1986), p. 63.
7. *Origins,* Volume 17, No. 16, October 1, 1987, p. 261.
8. Anne Roche Muggeridge, *The Desolate City* (San Francisco: Harper & Row Publishers, 1986), p. 9.
9. *Ibid.,* p. 44.
10. *Origins,* Volume 18, No. 7, June 30, 1988, pp. 97-101.
11. *Ibid.,* p. 100.
12. *Ibid.,* pp. 100-101.
13. Syracuse *Herald Journal,* June 30, 1988, pp. A-1, 6.
14. Charles E. Curran, *op. cit.,* pp. 3, 268.
15. *Ibid.,* p. 270.
16. *Vatican Council II,* edited by Austin Flannery, O.P. (Northport, NY: Costello Publishing Company, 1975), *Constitution on the Sacred Liturgy,* art. 59.

Chapter 2: The Process Called Conversion

1. David K. O'Rourke, *A Process Called Conversion* (Garden City, NY: Doubleday and Company, Inc., 1985), pp. 1-17.
2. *Ibid.,* pp. 16, 33.
3. *Rite of Christian Initiation of Adults,* No. 1.
4. *The New Catholics,* edited by Dan O'Neill (New York: Crossroad Publishing Company, 1987).
5. *Ibid.,* pp. 1-19.
6. *Ibid.,* p. 19.
7. *Ibid.,* p. 22.
8. *Ibid.*
9. James W. Fowler, *Becoming Adult, Becoming Christian,* "Adult Development and Christian Faith" (San Francisco: Harper & Row Publishers, 1984), pp. 52-71.
10. *Ibid.,* pp. 74, 75.
11. *The New Catholics,* p. 27.

12. Elisabeth Kübler-Ross, *On Death and Dying* (New York: Macmillan, 1969).
13. *Once a Catholic*, p. 302.
14. *Ibid.*, pp. 311-312.
15. *Ibid.*, p. 312.
16. See Andrew M. Greeley, *The Religious Imagination* (New York: William H. Sadlier, Inc., 1981), p. 107.
17. *Ibid.*, p. 149.
18. *Ibid.*
19. George Gallup, Jr. and Jim Castelli, *The American Catholic People: Their Beliefs, Practices and Values* (Garden City, NY: Doubleday and Company, Inc., 1987), pp. 28-29, 152-153.

Chapter 3: A Biblical Perspective

1. Raymond E. Brown, *The Community of the Beloved Disciple* (New York: Paulist Press, 1979), p. 185.
2. I am deeply indebted to Raymond E. Brown, S.S., professor of Sacred Scripture at Union Theological Seminary in New York City, and Rev. Michael Beers, professor of Old Testament studies at Mount Saint Mary's Seminary in Emmitsburg, Maryland, for their "jealous God" and "potter and clay" concepts as they relate to our study.
3. Exodus 20:5. See footnote of the NAB version.
4. *The Jerome Biblical Commentary* (Englewood Cliffs, NJ: Prentice-Hall, Inc., 1968), p. 57.
5. *Ibid.*, pp. 65-66.
6. *Ibid.*, p. 105. See also *The Book of Deuteronomy*. Part I with a commentary by George S. Glanzman, S.J. (New York: Paulist Press, 1960), pp. 16-17.
7. *The Jerome Biblical Commentary*, p. 441.
8. Isaiah 42:14. See footnote of the NAB version. Confer also *The Jerome Biblical Commentary*, p. 367.
9. *The Jerome Biblical Commentary*, pp. 370-371.
10. *Ibid.*, p. 317.
11. See footnote of the NAB version.
12. G.B. Caird, *The Gospel of St. Luke*. The Pelican New Testament Commentaries (Baltimore, MD: Penguin Books, Inc., 1975), p. 86.
13. See NAB footnote to Matthew 12:15-21.
14. J.C. Fenton, *The Gospel of St. Matthew*. The Pelican New Testament Commentaries (Baltimore, MD: Penguin Books, Inc., 1976), p. 195; John P. Meier, *Matthew* (Wilmington, DE: Michael Glazier, Inc., 1980), p. 132.
15. William Barclay, *The Gospel of Matthew: Volume 2*, The Daily Study Bible Series (Philadelphia: The Westminster Press, 1975), pp. 33-34.
16. *Ibid.*, p. 34.
17. William Barclay, *The Gospel of Matthew: Volume 2*, pp. 71-75; J.C. Fenton, *The Gospel of St. Matthew*, pp. 219-221; John P. Meier, *Matthew*, pp. 146-148; *The Jerome Biblical Commentary*, pp. 87-88; footnotes of the NAB version.

18. *Ibid.*
19. Barclay, pp. 88-90; Fenton, pp. 228-229; Meier, pp. 152-153; *The Jerome Biblical Commentary,* p. 88; footnotes of the NAB version.
20. G.B. Caird, *The Gospel of St. Luke,* pp. 179-181.
21. *Ibid.*

Chapter 4: The Cruel or Compassionate Church

1. Rev. John Catoir, "Is the Church Unforgiving?" *America,* January 19, 1985, p. 46. Direct quotes are from this article, which represented a development of reflections commemorating the 125th anniversary of the founding of the Congregation of St. Paul.
2. "Instruction on Respect for Human Life in its Origin and on the Dignity of Procreation: Replies to Certain Questions of the Day." Congregation for the Doctrine of the Faith, February 22, 1987.
3. David K. O'Rourke, O.P., "Revolution and Alienation in the American Church," *Commonweal,* February 11, 1983, pp. 76-79. Direct quotes are from this article.
4. *Ibid.,* p. 79.
5. Philip J. Murnion, "A Sacramental Church," *America,* March 25, 1983, pp. 226-228. Direct quotes are from this article.
6. I am indebted to two scholars in particular for their assistance with this section. Father Raymond E. Brown, S.S., helped with his description of the early churches the apostles left behind. Father Avery Dulles, S.J., professor of systematic theology at The Catholic University of America, was especially generous with his time, his advice and even his books.
7. John Paul II, *Reconciliation and Penance.* Post Synodal Apostolic Exhortation, December 2, 1984 (Washington, DC: USCC Office of Publishing and Promotion Services, 1984) section 34.
8. *Ibid.*
9. *Vatican Council II, Dogmatic Constitution on the Church,* art. 25.
10. *Vatican Council II, Decree on the Church's Missionary Activity,* art. 1-3.
11. John Paul II, *Reconciliation and Penance,* sec. 12.
12. John Paul II, *Rich in Mercy.* Encyclical, November 30, 1980 (Washington, DC: USCC Publications Office, 1981), Part VII, p. 41.
13. Avery Dulles, S.J., *The Reshaping of Catholicism* (San Francisco: Harper & Row Publishers, 1988); direct quotes are from pp. 96-109.
14. *Vatican Council II, Constitution on the Sacred Liturgy,* art. 59.
15. *Rite of Christian Initiation,* art. 1; 3-5, art. 7.
16. John Paul II, *The Christian Family in the Modern World (Familiaris Consortio).* Apostolic Exhortation, December 15, 1981 (Northport, NY: 1982), sec. 56.
17. *Ibid.,* sec. 67.
18. Avery Dulles, S.J., *Models of the Church: Expanded Version* (Garden City, NY: Image Books, 1987), pp. 66-67.
19. Mark Searle, "Ritual and Music: A Theory of Liturgy," *Church,* Fall 1986, pp. 48-52.
20. *Vatican Council II, Dogmatic Constitution on the Church,* chapters I-II.

21. Synod of Bishops, "The Final Report," 1.4, in *Origins*. vol. 15, no. 27, (Dec. 19, 1985), p. 445.

22. Avery Dulles, S.J., *Models of the Church: Expanded Version,* p. 206.

23. John Paul II, *Redemptor Hominis*. Encyclical, March 4, 1979 (Washington, DC: USCC Publications Office, 1979), no. 21, pp. 89-90.

24. Avery Dulles, S.J., *Models of the Church: Expanded Version,* chapter 13; *A Church to Believe In* (New York: Crossroad, 1982), chapter 1.

25. Avery Dulles, S.J., *A Church to Believe In,* p. 13.

26. Raymond E. Brown, S.S., *The Churches the Apostles Left Behind* (New York: Paulist Press, 1984), chapter 8.

27. *Ibid.,* pp. 132-133.

28. *Ibid.,* p. 141.

29. *Ibid.,* p. 145.

30. Avery Dulles, S.J., *A Church to Believe In,* p. 4.

31. Rev. Philip J. Murnion, "At the Center of the Church: The Parish," *Parish Ministry,* last issue, 1982, pp. 5, 10.

Chapter 5: Laws and Life

Note: I am very grateful to Samuel J.M. Donnelly, professor of law at the Syracuse University College of Law, and to Msgr. Frederick R. McManus, professor of canon law at The Catholic University of America, for their invaluable guidance in connection with this chapter. In addition, I wish to express my gratitude to Mrs. Rosemary K. Carr and Ms. Catherine F. Carr for their assistance in tracking down articles at the LeMoyne College library in Syracuse.

1. John Paul II, *Sacrae Disciplinae Leges*. Apostolic Constitution, January 25, 1983.

2. *Ibid.* The development of this comparison between secular and sacred law grew out of several conversations in August 1988, with Rev. Patrick J. O'Leary, J.D., of East Syracuse, New York.

3. *Code of Canon Law,* canon 1063.

4. *Syracuse Post-Standard,* August 16, 1988, p. B-1.

5. John Paul II, *Sacrae Disciplinae Leges.*

6. John A. Alesandro, "General Introduction," *The Code of Canon Law: A Text and Commentary,* edited by James A. Coriden, Thomas J. Green and Donald E. Heintschel (New York: Paulist Press, 1985), p. 13.

7. *Ibid.*

8. *Ibid.,* p. 11.

9. *Ibid.*

10. *Ibid.*

11. John M. Huels, O.S.M., *Liturgical Law: An Introduction* (Washington, DC: The Pastoral Press, 1987) pp. 10-11. This small, but very helpful book is the basic source for the material which follows about the varying kinds of liturgical laws.

12. *Ibid.,* p. 11.

13. *Code of Canon Law,* canon 849.

14. John M. Huels, O.S.M., *op. cit.,* p. 12.
15. *Ibid.,* pp. 12-14.
16. *Ibid.,* pp. 14-15.
17. *Ibid.,* p. 15.
18. *Ibid.* See also *Rite of Marriage.*
19. *Ibid.,* pp. 15-16.
20. *Ibid.,* p. 16.
21. *Code of Canon Law,* canon 872.
22. Frederick R. McManus, "Liturgical Law and Difficult Cases." *Worship,* volume 48 (1974), no. 6, pp. 347-366. This brilliant essay is the source behind my brief treatment of those avenues of relief from the law.
23. *Code of Canon Law,* canon 29 (1917), 27 (1983).
24. *Ibid.,* canons 85, 87, 90.
25. See NAB footnote to Philippians 4:5. Also William Barclay, *The Letters to the Philippians, Colossians and Thessalonians: Revised Edition* (Philadelphia: The Westminster Press, 1975), p. 75.
26. *Ibid.,* Barclay, p. 75.
27. Ladislas Orsy, S.J. "Book I-General Norms," *The Code of Canon Law: A Text and Commentary,* Notes, p. 42.
28. Frederick R. McManus, *op. cit.,* pp. 364-365.
29. John A. Alesandro, *op. cit.,* p. 13.
30. *Syracuse Post-Standard.* August 16, 1988, p. A-2.
31. John M. Huels, O.S.M., *op. cit.,* p. 17.
32. *Vatican Council II, Constitution on the Sacred Liturgy,* art. 22.
33. Thomas Richstatter, O.F.M., *Liturgical Law: New Style, New Spirit* (Chicago: Franciscan Herald Press, 1977), pp. 161-180. R. Kevin Seasolta, *New Liturgy, New Laws* (Collegeville, MN: The Liturgical Press, 1979), pp. 202-211.
34. Lon L. Fuller, *Anatomy of the Law* (New York: Frederick A. Praeger, Publishers, 1968), p. 53.
35. *Ibid.,* p. 85.
36. *Ibid.*
37. H.L.A. Hart, *The Concept of Law,* chapter VII, pp. 121-132; Samuel J.M. Donnelly, Book Review, *Hofstra Law Review,* vol. 3, no. 3. Summer, 1975, pp. 899-919.

Chapter 6: A Warm Welcome

1. David K. O'Rourke, *A Process Called Conversion,* p. 159.
2. Christopher Lasch, *The Culture of Narcissism* (New York: Warner Books, 1979). See especially pp. 315-317; 369-397.
3. John Paul II, *The Christian Family in the Modern World,* no. 66.
4. Thornton and Freedman, "The Changing American Family," *Population Reference Bureau Bulletin,* October 1983, pp. 7-8.
5. "National Vital Statistics Report," Center for Disease Control and Prevention, March 9, 2000.

6. Arthur J. Norton, and Louisa F. Miller, *Marriage, Divorce and Remarriage in the 1990's*, U.S. Department of Commerce, Economics and Statistics Administration, Bureau of the Census, Current Population Reports, Special Studies #P23-180.

7. Cathleen Crowell Webb and Marie Chaplan, *Forgive Me* (Old Tappan, NJ: Fleming H. Revell Company, 1985), pp. 22-23.

8. Robert Bauman, *The Gentleman from Maryland: The Conscience of a Gay Conservative* (New York: Arbor House, 1986).

9. Judith Viorst, *Necessary Losses* (New York: Fawcett Gold Medal Books, 1987), p. 3.

10. *Preparing for Marriage: A Study of Marriage Preparation in American Catholic Dioceses* (St. Meinrad, Indiana: Abbey Press, 1983).

11. David K. O'Rourke, O.P., "Unfair Assessments: Obstacles for Engaged Couples," *Church,* Fall 1985, pp. 24-26.

12. I am grateful to Rev. Neal Quartier, M.S.W., for his suggestions on this issue.

13. Charles L. Whitfield, M.D. *Healing the Child Within* (Health Communications, Inc.: Deerfield Beach, FL, 1987), pp. 68, 70, 72, 71.

14. Judith Viorst, *Necessary Losses,* p. 366.

15. *Ibid.,* pp. 2-3.

16. Paul VI, *On the Regulation of Birth.* Encyclical, July 25, 1968, art. 29.

17. Paul VI, *Evangelization in the Modern World.* Encyclical, December 8, 1975 (Washington, DC: USCC Office of Publishing and Promotion Services, 1975), p. 15.

18. Garrison Keillor, *Lake Wobegon Days* (New York: Penguin Books, 1987), pp. 309-310.

Chapter 8: Baptism: Pastoral Suggestions

1. "A Quest for Baptism," *The Church World* (Portland, ME), April 7, 1983, p. 28.

2. *Rite of Baptism for Children,* no. 105.

3. *Ibid.,* no. 82. *Instruction on Infant Baptism,* no. 29.

4. *Vatican Council II, Dogmatic Constitution on the Church,* no. 33.

5. *Ibid., Decree on the Apostolate of Lay People,* no. 11.

6. *Rite of Christian Initiation,* "General Introduction," no. 7.

7. St. Ignatius Loyola Church, 2300 Burnhamthorpe Road West, Mississauga, Toronto, Canada LSL 2E3, Rev. Desmond O'Neill, pastor.

8. The Liturgical Press, Collegeville, Minnesota, produces a complete series of items explaining the sacrificial giving concept including a manual, a pamphlet, leaflets, children's envelopes, and audio-visual materials.

9. *Code of Canon Law,* canons 102, 107, 98, 857.

10. *Ibid.,* canons 857, 859, 860.

11. *Vatican Council II, Constitution on the Sacred Liturgy,* no. 10.

12. *Code of Canon Law,* canons 897-899, 1246-1248.

13. John Naisbitt, *Megatrends* (New York: Warner Books, 1984).

14. *Instruction on Infant Baptism,* no. 30-31; *Code of Canon Law,* canon 868.
15. *Ibid.,* no. 31.
16. *Rite of Baptism for Children,* no. 9.

Chapter 10: Marriage: Pastoral Suggestions

1. Many of the ideas, statistics and comments in this chapter can be found in *Faithful to Each Other Forever: A Catholic Handbook of Pastoral Help for Marriage Preparation,* a massive document and project of the Bishops' Committee for Pastoral Research and Practices of the National Conference of Catholic Bishops in the United States, an effort in which I was heavily involved.
2. John Paul II, *The Christian Family in the Modern World,* no. 66.
3. *Ibid.*
4. *Ibid.,* no. 68.
5. David K. O'Rourke, O.P., "Unfair Assessments: Obstacles for Engaged Couples," p. 24.
6. St. Maria Goretti Roman Catholic Church, 6261 North Granite Reef Road, Scottsdale, Arizona 85253, Rev. John D. Spaulding, Pastor.
7. Joseph M. Champlin, *Together for Life* (Notre Dame, IN: Ave Maria Press, 1970, latest revised edition, 1996). Regular and Outside Mass formats.
8. Some priests and pastoral ministers have found the illustrated *What It Means to Be Catholic* (Los Angeles: Franciscan Communications, 1986) helpful in lieu of an actual series of instructions.
9. John Paul II, *The Christian Family in the Modern World,* no. 69.
10. *Code of Canon Law,* canon 1060.

ST PAULS

This book was designed and published by ST PAULS/ Alba House, the publishing arm of the Society of St. Paul, an international religious congregation of priests and brothers dedicated to serving the Church through the communications media. For information regarding this and associated ministries of the Pauline Family of Congregations, write to the Vocation Director, Society of St. Paul, 7050 Pinehurst, Dearborn, Michigan 48126. Phone (313) 582-3798 or check our internet site, www.albahouse.org